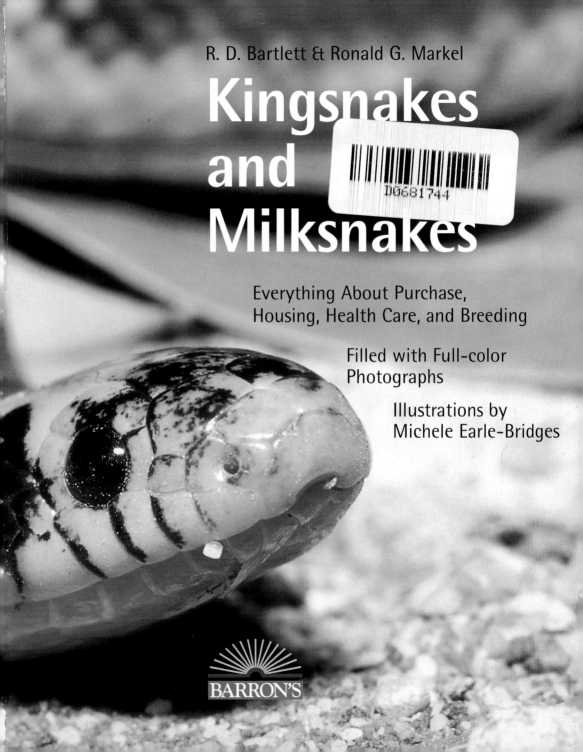

R. D. Bartlett & Ronald G. Markel

Kingsnakes and Milksnakes

Everything About Purchase,
Housing, Health Care, and Breeding

Filled with Full-color
Photographs

Illustrations by
Michele Earle-Bridges

D0681744

BARRON'S

2 CONTENTS

UNDERSTANDING KINGSNAKES AND MILKSNAKES

Snakes have survived to the present day with minimal changes. However, attitudes toward snakes certainly have changed over the past several decades.

Attitudes

Through the centuries, myths about snakes have coupled fear with fascination. The same people who claim to loathe snakes—those cold-blooded serpents that slither around on their bellies—are the same folks who stand in line at the zoo reptile house to view the very creatures they fear.

Snake symbols date back to ancient civilizations but are familiar today, too. The staff of Aesculapius (with a single snake) and the symbol of caduceus (with two intertwining snakes) are readily recognized insignias of the medical profession.

Today, herpetology is a hobby increasing in popularity with people of both sexes, of all ages, and from all walks of life. Public awareness and education, television, and books that

This is a bicolored Honduran milksnake.

are readily available have all contributed to the acceptance of and interest in these creatures.

Evolution

Some 340 million years ago, during the Carboniferous period, after having evolved from the amphibians, reptiles ruled the world. There were many distinct groups at that time. Some forms were not terribly different from those seen today. Lizards, for example, were and are readily recognized as lizards.

After first appearing, reptiles began to diversify. During the Mesozoic era (230 to 70 million years ago) flying reptiles appeared. Many reptiles then returned to the seas and lakes, and dinosaurs dominated the land.

Because they are not as dependent on water as amphibians, reptiles have more successfully colonized many areas of the world. This is especially true of arid land where the more specialized eggs of reptiles have adapted well. Unlike the easily desiccated gelatinous eggs of amphibia, reptiles produce parchment or hard-shelled eggs that are less moisture permeable.

About 140 million years ago, during the Cretaceous period, snakes evolved. They have survived through the Paleocene period to the present with minimal changes.

Besides the snake group, which contains about 2,400 species, only three other families (divided into four groups) of reptiles have survived the trials of the ages and are alive today.

The largest and most diverse of these are lizards, with about 3,000 species. Turtles are next, with about 200 species. The remaining two groups, crocodilians and *rhynchocephalians* (tuataras) are much smaller. The crocodilians have a total of 23 species, and primitive lizard-like creatures known as tuataras (or "beak-heads") have only two.

Snakes live in all but the very coldest areas of the world. Their long, slender body form is unmistakable. At best, they have only vestiges of limbs (boas and pythons). There are three major groups of snakes:

✔ *Henophidia*, a group that encompasses primitive snakes, such as boas, pythons, and pipe snakes;

✔ *Scolecophidia*, containing the many families of blind snakes; and

✔ *Caenophidia*, the members of which are often referred to as advanced snakes. Within this last family we find the majority of the extant snakes, ranging from harmless water and kingsnakes to the potentially deadly cobras, sea snakes, and vipers.

Anatomy

The extremely flexible spine of the snake contains from 180 vertebrae in the smaller species to more than 400 in the larger ones. The side-to-side movement most commonly used by snakes is referred to as "serpentine movement." This movement requires powerful trunk muscles and a strong back.

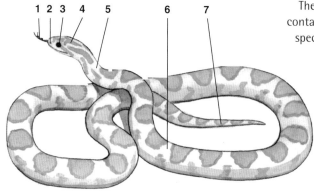

General anatomy of the snake.
1. Tongue, 2. Nostril, 3. Eye,
4. Head, 5. Neck, 6. Body, 7. Tail

Snakes also have very strong vertebrae to maintain the stress and strain that is placed on the backbone by the muscles.

Jaws: Because a snake's upper and lower jawbones are attached to the more rigid skull only by muscles and ligament, a snake is able to consume proportionately large prey. The jaws stretch not only from top to bottom but from side to side as well, allowing a snake to swallow prey much larger than its own girth.

Throat: The throat or gullet makes up one-third of the snake's entire length. This leads to a very long stomach that, like the gullet, can stretch to accommodate large food. Since it has been found with captive snakes that two or three small prey items are better than a single large one, captives are seldom fed oversized meals. This is not always the case in the wild where available prey size cannot be monitored.

Internal organs: The other internal organs of a snake are also elongated and fit one behind the other. Although snakes are often referred to as deaf, this is not at all the case. Despite lacking external ears and the fact that the single earbone is attached to the jaw rather than a tympanic membrane, snakes are able to hear low-frequency sounds quite well. They are also able to perceive and interpret ground vibrations.

Tongue: As it flicks in and out, the forked tongue of a snake "tastes" scent particles both in the air and on the ground. If a snake's tongue is not actively checking the environment, it could be a sign of an unhealthy specimen.

Internal organs of a kingsnake or milksnake.
1. Windpipe, 2. Liver, 3. Heart, 4. Left lung,
5. Right lung, 6. Pancreas, 7. Gallbladder,
8. Small Intestine, 9. Stomach, 10. Left
kidney, 11. Large intestine, 12. Rectum

Jacobson's organ: Once the scent particles are encountered they are transmitted to the vomeronasal (the Jacobson's) organ in the roof of the mouth. There the collected chemical cues are analyzed. Such diverse things as prey types and trails, approaching enemies, and mate receptivity can be instantly determined by these sensitive organs.

Skin

The dry (not slimy) scaly skin of the reptile forms a protective barrier between the internal tissues and the outside environment. The skin also helps prevent desiccation and injury from accident or predators. Considering the fact that ectothermic (formerly referred to as "cold-blooded") snakes survive a variety of harsh

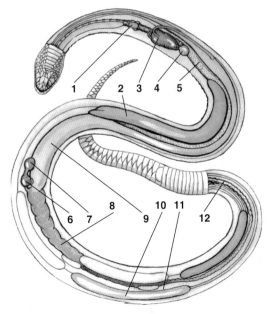

environmental elements, the scaly skin does an excellent job of protecting the animal.

Keratin: The scales consist of a proteinaceous material called keratin. Keratin is similar in makeup to the material that forms animal claws and human fingernails.

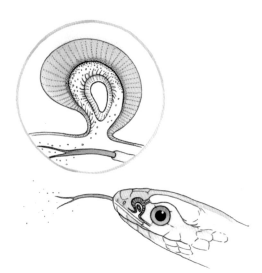

A banded albino California kingsnake.

Shedding

The keratinous epidermis of the snake being basically inert, is periodically outgrown. When this occurs the snake sheds its skin (see page 54). Young, rapidly growing snakes shed more frequently than older snakes that are growing more slowly.

The shedding is triggered by hormonal action. As the old skin separates from the new skin forming beneath it, a blue translucency obscures normal coloration and, since the eye-protecting brille (spectacle) is involved, impedes the snake's vision. At this time snakes often become inactive and secretive. Once the new skin is completely formed, the snake sheds the old one.

Illustration of the Jacobson's organ, which is how snakes sense with their tongues. This is especially important when foraging for food items.

The hatchlings of many kingsnakes have red overtones on the sides. This is an Apalachicola Lowland kingsnake.

This eastern kingsnake from western Georgia has an aberrant pattern.

An aberrant tangerine Honduran milksnake.

Hobbyists are now producing many hybrid snakes. This is a gray-banded x Arizona mountain kingsnake hybrid.

━━━ T I P ━━━

On the Move

People often exaggerate about how fast a snake moves. Few move faster than we would during a brisk walk, but snakes are infinitely more at home than we are in rough terrain. Catching an alert specimen in its natural habitat can be quite a challenge.

To begin the shedding process the snake rubs its snout against a rough object, freeing the already loosened old skin from the lips and snout. Pressing its snout against the substrate (or other anchoring point) the snake then slowly crawls forward and out of its inverting old skin. The process of shedding is also

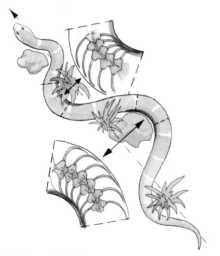

This is called the serpentine movement and illustrates forward motion in kingsnakes and milksnakes.

referred to as molting, sloughing, or, scientifically, as ecdysis. Problems related to shedding are discussed in detail in another chapter.

Locomotion

Despite being legless, snakes are quite agile. Their basic form of locomotion is much the same no matter how divergent the snake species. Almost all movements—sidewinding of specialized desert species, swimming of the paddle-tailed sea snakes, or climbing of the prehensile-tailed palm vipers—are slight variations of the same side-to-side serpentine motion. Some snakes, especially those that are heavy bodied but have well-developed ventral scales may occasionally use a nonserpentine, rectilinear ("caterpillar") mode of progression.

The side-to-side, wavelike motion of serpentine progression propels the snake in a forward direction. The motion is accomplished by the repeated relaxation and contraction of selected muscles. The pressing of the body waves and ventral scales against the irregularities of the substrate or surrounding objects is what moves the snake forward. When the surface on which a snake is placed has few or no irregularities (such as a sheet of glass), the snake has a difficult time moving.

Eyesight

Most snakes have rather well-developed eyesight. Most readily see movement. Whether they perceive stationary objects or shapes is debatable. The combination of vibrations, odors, and movement produced by the snake's prey and enemies enables it to detect the prey, compensating for any lack of visual acuity.

Dorsal view of scales on the top of the head.
1. Parietal, 2. Postocular, 3. Frontal,
4. Preocular, 5. Loreal, 6. Internasal,
7. Rostral, 8. Temporal, 9. Upper labial,
10. Supraocular, 11. Prefrontal, 12. Nasal

At one time snakes were thought to be able to hypnotize their prey (and people!) and render them motionless. The continuous stare of the snake's lidless eyes is undoubtedly the origin of such a tale. These myths and legends have been passed on for centuries.

Although there is certainly no proof that such hypnotism can occur, perhaps a person or a potential meal could be immobilized by fear when they suddenly sense the presence of a snake. Often a snake will not react to the presence of a still person or creature until the latter assumes motion.

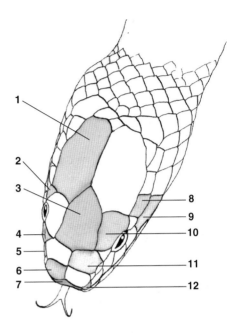

Life Span

A "normal" span of life for snakes in the wild is difficult to estimate because so many variables are involved. Nearly any figure mentioned is just a guess. Certainly where there is plenty of food and the snake is left alone or largely protected from predators (such as in the environs of a barn), a wild snake may survive for years.

The life span of a captive snake is another matter. Captive snakes are usually maintained in a sterile parasite/disease-free environment. They have a constant food supply and controlled cage conditions that, together, could most definitely extend a snake's life span for many additional years. Documented life spans for captive kingsnakes and milksnakes exceed 20 years. Healthy captives, which begin breeding at two to three years of age, are often still

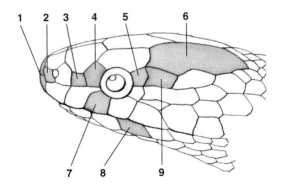

Scales on the side of the head help in identification of subspecies.
1. Rostal, 2. Nasal, 3. Loreal, 4. Preocular,
5. Postocular, 6. Parietal, 7. Upper labial,
8. Lower labial, 9. Temporal

An adult male Florida kingsnake.

This is a juvenile of the widespread and common eastern milksnake.

Dixon's milksnake has very broad red bands.

The San Bernardino mountain kingsnake is large and precisely patterned.

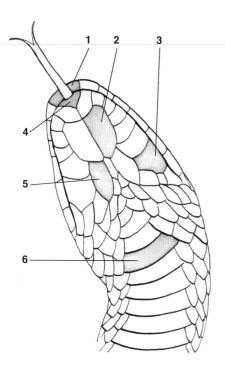

very well studied and documented since it was first described in the 1600s. The information contained in this book is current. We have commented on all available new information on certain taxa and have incorporated all valid nomenclatural information.

Distribution

Kingsnakes and milksnakes are distributed widely through the Americas. They range southward from southeastern Canada through much of the United States, Mexico, and Central America, to Ecuador, Colombia, and Venezuela in northern South America.

Scales

Lampropeltis is derived from the Greek *lampros*, meaning "shiny," and *pelta,* which means "scales" or "shields." Together, these Greek words translate to "shiny scales." The scales in which the milksnakes and kingsnakes are clad are smooth (not keeled), and each scale bears two apical pits (tiny sensory depressions). Although the subcaudal scales are divided, the anal plate of the members of this genus is single.

Classification

The following is an example of how a Florida kingsnake would be scientifically classified:
- Class: Reptilia
- Order: Squamata
- Suborder: Serpentes
- Family: Colubridae

being bred 10 or 12 years later. Under ideal conditions a captive kingsnake or milksnake may be expected to live (and often to breed) for 15 or more years.

Natural History and Taxonomy

Although the natural histories of kingsnakes and milksnakes are well documented, there has been some taxonomic instability in recent years. Still, in contrast with the paucity of information available on some snakes, the members of this snake genus are well understood, and information about them is readily accessible.

The genus *Lampropeltis,* which is comprised solely of kingsnakes and milksnakes, has been

- Sub-family: Colubrinae
- Genus: *Lampropeltis*
- Species: *getula*
- Subspecies: *floridana*

Habitats

The widely distributed kingsnakes and milk-snakes can be found in most habitats (there are no truly aquatic species), from below sea level to the peaks of some of the highest mountains. These snakes may be encountered in arid savannas, deserts, mountains, prairies, marsh-lands, forests, and rain forests.

Identification

Milksnakes and kingsnakes are, like all crea-tures, identified by a number of morphological features.

✔ Kingsnakes and milksnakes are snakes of small to moderate size that have rather short tails.

✔ The size of the members of this genus ranges from 16 inches to 6 feet (41 cm to 2 m).

✔ Dorsal scale rows at midbody range from 17 to 27.

✔ The hemipenes (male copulatory organs) may be either distinctly or shallowly (and asymmetrically) bilobed.

✔ Scale colors and patterns vary by subspecies.

Size and Rate of Growth

Estimating the size of a snake in its natural habitat is difficult. Estimating the age of an adult wild snake is almost impossible. To sur-vive in the wild, snakes must become masters at concealment. Many remain motionless even

TIP

Identifying a Species

When you are attempting to identify a species or subspecies of snake, the scale-row count can be extremely important. An accu-rate count of the scale rows is most easily obtained from a shed skin. The number of scale rows present at mid-body (dorsally), on the belly (ventrally), and beneath the tail (subcaudally) are often especially important when identifying questionable species.

when closely approached. Others glide quickly away. Whichever the method, those snakes that are the most successful in evading detection live longest.

It is somewhat easier to guess the age of hatchling or juvenile snakes in natural habitat. Their size and the time of year that they are seen offer clues. For instance, you can usually guess that a juvenile snake (12 inches [30 cm] or less in length) found in the late summer or early fall is a hatchling. A snake twice that size is probably a yearling. Beyond this size you can only guess the snake's age.

A snake grows fastest during its first year of life. During this time, snakes are the most defenseless and have the highest mortality rate. In their efforts to avoid predators, baby snakes remain concealed much of the time. Snakes continue to grow, although more slowly, after attaining sexual maturity. Snakes with a readily available food source grow more quickly than those that eat only sporadically. Snakes grow little, if any, during hibernation.

CONSIDERATIONS AND PREPARATIONS

Before you buy any snake, check with your local animal control agency to find out what laws govern the ownership of snakes. Not all communities have the same regulations, so check before you buy.

Considerations Before You Buy

In many areas of the country, keeping exotic pets is regulated by various laws—and snakes are usually considered "exotic." It may be necessary to acquire city, county, state, or even federal permits to legally possess or transport certain species. In addition to your local animal control agency, most local pet stores know the regulations and can assist you. Before you buy, consider your responses to the following questions:

✔ What are the reasons behind your purchase of a snake?

✔ Do you merely want a pet?

✔ Are you planning to breed the specimens?

✔ Is this the first of several that you are planning to buy over a period of time?

Termed "disappearing pattern Honduran" the color contrasts on this milksnake fade with advancing age.

Sex: A single male snake (often the cheapest to purchase) makes a fine pet. Although females are equally good, they are often much more expensive; and since many herpetoculturists are reluctant to part with females, that sex may not be as readily available, especially in larger sizes.

Generally more females are available after the breeding season than at other times of year. However, even then, with some of the more rarely seen forms, breeders may be reluctant to sell single females. Instead they may require the purchase of a pair.

Deposit: Some subspecies of milksnakes and kingsnakes may be so much in demand that they are available only by early reservation. Many breeders require a deposit in advance to reserve the baby or babies. A deposit for the hatchlings may be required even before the breeding season has started.

Juveniles: Raising juvenile milksnakes and kingsnakes can be rewarding. It is enjoyable to watch your specimens grow from hatchling to

TIP

Responsibility

Remember, snakes, like any other captive or pet animal, rely on you for their well-being! You must take this responsibility seriously.

breeding adult. It can also be frustrating, especially if your hatchlings turn out to be poor feeders.

Price: Generally, snakes that are captive-bred, established feeders will demand a higher price. In the long run this may be well worth the difference in price. Breeding loans of higher-priced snakes are not uncommon. Details of the agreement are usually set when the eggs hatch and the sex ratio of the babies is determined.

Concerns for the Potential Snake Keeper

Before purchasing your snake determine whether you can provide the clean, safe, secure environment that is necessary to ensure the specimen's well-being. You must also be willing to explore and fulfill all legal obligations and to be able to afford any recurring expenses (permits, food, bedding, and so on).

The acquisition of your milksnake or kingsnake should be the result of careful consideration, not impulse. If this is your first snake, have you considered all of the pros and cons of keeping a snake in captivity? There is much to think about. Let's explore a few more aspects.

✔ When querying about permits, be sure to also question whether a maximum number or size limitations apply.

✔ Are pet deposits required by your landlord? Does your lease (if applicable) allow the keeping of snakes?

✔ Can you provide the conditions necessary for the well-being of the animal? Can you properly hibernate a snake if necessary? Is there sufficient space for the proper caging?

✔ Have you considered all recurring and initial expenses, including such things as purchase of the specimen, caging, heating, water facilities, and a security system?

✔ Is a constant food source available, either through purchase or breeding of food rodents?

✔ Is there any family conflict about your keeping of snakes?

✔ Maintaining a clean, healthy environment for your snake takes time. Are you willing to make the sacrifice?

Choosing a Healthy Snake

Milksnakes and kingsnakes are commonly kept by both casual hobbyists and dedicated herpetoculturists. Whether you are new to the hobby or an old pro, here are a few suggestions that that might make your choice of a healthy specimen easier.

Physical Appearance

The physical appearance of your prospective animal is an excellent indicator of its health. A basic physical examination is simple and can avoid costly veterinary bills in the future. Consider not only the condition of the animal in which you are interested, but the overall condition of all of the animals at the facility where you will purchase your snake.

• The animal should be in good condition, alert, fairly strong, and of proper weight. Gross obesity can be as deleterious to health as malnutrition.

• Never choose a snake that is lethargic and lacks muscle tone. When a snake is disturbed it should actively protrude and withdraw its tongue, flicking it up and down when it is extended. When a snake is lifted, it should either actively try to escape or coil tightly around the hand and arm of the person who is supporting it. It should not dangle limply or move spastically or with difficulty.

• Check carefully for respiratory distress. Do not purchase a snake that is wheezing or gasping for breath. Bubbling when exhaling or a nasal discharge are also indications of respiratory infection. Snakes showing either symptom should be avoided.

• Check the snake's mouth. Gently repress the lip, or open the mouth and check gum and tissue color. This should appear clean and whitish or pinkish. The presence of any yellow, cheesy substance, swelling, or other discolorations and abnormalities can indicate a serious, even potentially fatal, expensive to treat infection or injury.

• How does the snake's skin look? It should be clean, shiny, and devoid of lumps, bumps, wounds, sores, blisters, and scars. Look for mites on and under the scales, around the eyes, or in the nostril and mouth area.

Feeding Characteristics

If the snake you are interested in is in a pet store, ask to see it feed. If it is from a reptile dealer/breeder whom you know to be reliable, ask for feeding characteristics or peculiarities.

Is the snake feeding on mice? Will it only accept lizards? Is it a voracious feeder or is it reluctant to eat unless conditions are ideal? Ask questions. Avoid buying a snake from a dealer or company whom you do not know or for whom you cannot obtain references.

If the snake is a baby—most affordably priced snakes are—be certain that you have proper food available. A baby milksnake or kingsnake will want newly born pinkie mice or even small lizards. These must be available to you on a regular basis.

Most reputable breeders and dealers offer some form of guarantee on the health of the purchased specimen. This might be in the form of refund, exchange, or replacement if problems occur within a given time period (often 10 days). If such a guarantee is not offered, go elsewhere.

Ordering a Snake from a Distant Company

Shippers have become very familiar with the several methods now available to transport harmless snakes. Overnight, door-to-door service is now available except on holidays and Sundays. Check with your shipper for all shipping details including the transportation company used and a shipment tracking number. Also discuss the shipper's live delivery policy. After the shipment is en route, its positioning and expected delivery time can be tracked online at your convenience.

Preparing the Cage

Your terrarium or cage should be completely ready before you bring the snake home. The cage top must be sufficiently tight and secure

The bluish overtones on this young black milksnake are caused by an impending shed.

A banded normal California kingsnake.

A banded lavender albino California kingsnake.

The Sierra mountain kingsnake is a common and beautiful creature.

This pretty hatchling Florida kingsnake is from south Florida.

The hatchlings of many kingsnakes have red overtones on the sides. This is an Apalachicola Lowland kingsnake.

to prevent escape. If you spend $50 or $100 on a snake, you don't want to wake up some morning and find it gone.

Snakes of all kinds are escape artists, but this is particularly true of milksnakes and kingsnakes. Burrowers by nature, milksnakes and kingsnakes will push and shove at cage junctures—where the glass front slides into place, at the top of the cage where the top rests. If all is not very secure, they will escape.

Make sure the cage furniture and water dish cannot shift position and injure your snake should it push against it or attempt to hide beneath it. Have hiding spots safely arranged in the cage. Milksnakes and kingsnakes are hiders. It is especially important to them to be able to secure themselves in a new and unknown cage. Finally, make sure the water dish is big enough for the snake to get into—snakes need water to drink and to soak in.

Settling In

Once in the cage, give your new snake a few days to settle in before handling, feeding, or otherwise disturbing it. And if the meals you are feeding are large ones (making a considerable bulge in the snake's body when first eaten), do not handle the snake until the meal is well digested. To do so may cause regurgitation. This in turn can create other problems. Using prudence at the forefront can save time and prevent problems later.

Housing Your Snake Securely

Whether you have a store-purchased, lock-type aquarium, or a homemade cage, be

absolutely certain that it is secure. Never underestimate the ability of a snake to escape its confines.

Plastic Boxes

Plastic shoe, sweater, or blanket boxes are used as cages by many breeders of kingsnakes and milksnakes. These receptacles are lightweight, portable, easy to clean, and stackable when not in use. There are several manufacturers of such plastic boxes, making this type of inexpensive caging available from coast to coast. Drilling holes (or melting holes with a small soldering iron) in the sides of plastic receptacles provides adequate ventilation.

Pegboard Shelves

Some herpetoculturists use pegboard shelving units. They space the shelves closely together so that each shelf serves as the lid of the plastic boxes on the shelf below. When built correctly this negates the need for using the boxes' plastic covers while providing sufficient ventilation for the specimens. The drawback with these shelves is that some nervous specimens may actually "explode" out of the box into your face or onto the floor, as the container is removed from the shelf for cleaning or placement of food or fresh water. This can be disconcerting for both keeper and snake. The solution to the problem of nervous specimens is to have your cage-cleaning materials, including a holding bucket, near the caging.

Terraria

If you intend to display specimens, you may want to invest in a more elaborate, nicer looking setup. True terraria or commercial caging is available, but it is much more expensive than the plastic boxes. The objective is to provide yourself with ease of care while allowing suitable roominess for each and every specimen. Because of their cannibalistic tendencies, it is necessary to house each milksnake and kingsnake separately.

Substrates

Easily cleaned and replaced substrates such as pine, aspen, and folded newspapers are suitable. Because of the chemical compounds it contains, cedar shavings should be avoided. It is probably best not to even use cedar bedding for feed rodents. Aquarium gravel may look nice but has many drawbacks. Not only can it cause intestinal impactions if it is accidently ingested by the snakes, but it also needs to be thoroughly washed periodically, thoroughly dried before again being used, and is very heavy.

There are advantages and disadvantages to all substrates. What you finally settle on will depend on what is available and how many specimens you have. Cleanliness should always take precedence over prettiness. It takes time to maintain intricate and beautiful terraria. Most snake keepers opt for one or two display terraria and enjoy the practicality of the plastic boxes for nondisplay specimens. Keeping all specimens clean, warm, dry, and healthy is the priority.

Record Keeping

Keeping accurate records is an important aspect of reptile husbandry. Having all information pertinent to a particular specimen at your fingertips will help you track whatever idiosyncrasies are displayed by that specimen. Record-keeping cards, homemade or commercially

T I P

Protection in Transit

If the weather is cold, protect the snake you have purchased. Put it in a cloth bag, and put the bag inside your shirt while you transport it. Your body heat will give the snake the warmth it needs. If the snake is shipped to you in cold weather by a reliable dealer, he or she will enclose a heat-pack (a chemical hand warmer) to offset any chill.

purchased (cards are printed commercially for this very use—they are advertised in the classified sections of reptile magazines), should be kept for every specimen and should be started with the very first specimen you own. Three by five index cards should suffice with pertinent information, such as when and from where you acquired the specimen, feeding information (such as what was accepted and what was refused), when the snake begins and completes its shed cycle, and the size, weight, sex, species, and subspecies of the specimen. Records must also list any illnesses sustained by any specimen and the medication used to combat that illness. Breeding, egg laying and hatching dates, clutch sizes, the number of viable eggs in each clutch, and any special problems should also be noted.

All such data may be valuable when future breeding projects are considered. Keeping the cards easily accessible and a writing implement close at hand will make record keeping much more tenable. While keeping mental notes may work for a specimen or two, information isn't as easily remembered when a large number of specimens is involved.

These two simple shoebox cages each contain a Mexican milksnake.

Boards and other debris are favored hiding areas of red milksnakes and other subspecies.

All races of the Sonoran mountain kingsnake (Arizona mountain kingsnake pictured) have white snouts.

Hobbyists refer to this form of the variable kingsnake as the "mex-mex" phase.

Hatchling black milksnakes are intensely ringed in black, red, and white.

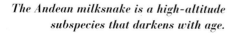

The Andean milksnake is a high-altitude subspecies that darkens with age.

Cage Use

Numerous cage designs are available commercially. Some are quite expensive, some are less so, but few are cheap. Whether your collection will be solely for enjoyment or you intend to enter the realm of commercial snake breeders should be decided early on, because this might determine the kind of caging you purchase.

If you wish to keep only a few specimens for pets or display, you may invest a little more in the aesthetics of your cages than if your long-term goal is to have a large breeding collection. You may opt to combine the two, having a few intricately designed display cages and a multitude of more functional breeding cages.

Display Tanks

Lock-top aquaria are often used for individual displays or the smaller collections of individuals who place a premium on aesthetics. Within these display tanks, cage furniture, such as rocks, bark, an attractive substrate, and even suitable live plants may be used. Above-tank lighting (mandatory if live plants are in the display) may add both beauty and a source of heat.

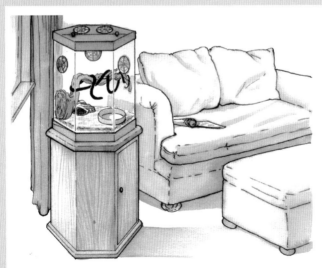

A very nice cage design for housing one specimen.

If you intend to expand your collection to several snakes, then perhaps a multicage unit would be best.

Plastic Boxes

The larger your collection, the more time and energy it will take to maintain it. With an increasing collection often comes a desire for more easily maintained caging. For this, several sizes of plastic boxes (shoe, sweater, blanket) have proven ideal. They are lightweight and stackable, have no sharp corners in which mites can hide, and are inexpensive. Shelving units can be easily constructed to hold several of these boxes, and different sizes can be incorporated into a single shelf. These boxes are also readily available at most large discount stores.

Smaller races of milksnakes and kingsnakes, or the babies of large ones, can be kept separately in the small boxes. As growth occurs the snake can be moved up to the next larger size. Of course, large blanket boxes are best for the larger forms of *Lampropeltis*.

Thermal Regulation

Snakes are ectothermic (cold-blooded) creatures. Since ectothermic animals lack internal body temperature regulatory mechanisms, you, the keeper, must provide them with the temperatures optimum to their well-being. A body temperature of between 80 and 85°F (26.7–29.4°C) is optimum for most milksnakes and kingsnakes. A few montane subspecies may prefer temperatures a few degrees cooler.

Thermostatic control: If you maintain a complete collection in one room, thermostatically controlling the room temperature will often suffice. Such thermostatic control will allow summer regulation to optimum warmth and also allow a winter cooling to a proper winter brumating (hibernating) temperature. For the latter, temperatures between 48 and 56°F (9–13°C) for a period of 60 to 80 days is suggested.

Heating devices: Several devices are available to heat individual cages. Among these are under-cage heating pads, blankets, or tapes, heat rocks, and above-tank lighting systems. No matter which type of individual tank heater you choose, it is suggested that you provide a thermal gradient within the terrarium. By so doing, your snake can choose the temperature that it prefers at any given time. The intensity of heat provided can be regulated by using an in-line rheostat or similar type of device.

Heat tapes: Heat tapes of several lengths are available. These are convenient to use when attempting to heat several terraria. When the tape is laid flat on a shelf, one end of several lined-up terraria can be set on the tape and heated.

As with caging, determine which type of heating device best suits your needs before making your purchase. Ask the opinions of other hobbyists. Profit from their experience. Your snakes need to be kept comfortable.

A simple stick-on thermometer to check and maintain the cage's temperature is important to avoid health problems, which can be caused by overheating or keeping the temperature too low.

Cages and Racks

Reptile cages, individually and as space-saving rack systems, are readily available in pet stores, herp expos, and online. Many of these are simply aquaria modified with screened or grated air vents and lockable sliding tops. However, others are formulated of "new age" scratch resistant plastics, vinyls, and acrylics and are quite elaborate. To prevent scratching and discoloration, special cleaning techniques may be needed on the transparent components of acrylic cages. Follow cleaning instructions carefully. Rack systems are designed to hold many plastic and acrylic cages. None of these racked caging systems are inexpensive, but most are neat, tidy, and allow easy access and remarkable security to cages, even when tiered. Although many rack and cage manufacturers advertise online, keep in mind that the cost of shipping one of these racks can add substantially to the overall expense.

FEEDING

Because they are nonspecialized feeders, kingsnakes and milksnakes are among the easiest snakes to maintain in captivity.

Food Supply

If you do not intend to breed your own supply of feed rodents, you must find a reliable and continuously available source before bringing your snakes home. Identify your primary food source and a secondary one, in case the first gives out. There are many reputable suppliers of both live and frozen mice across the United States. It is more expensive to have live mice shipped to you than frozen ones. Thus, if your snake will accept frozen mice, once they are thawed and warmed, they would certainly be an acceptable and more economical substitute.

Some snakes may take warmed dead mice with no reluctance whatsoever. However, there are snakes that require a little coaxing. Several methods have been successfully used to induce reluctant snakes to accept dead mice.

1. One is to feed your snake several small mice in succession, with only the first being

A pretty tangerine phase Honduran milksnake.

alive. Once the snake's hunting and feeding responses have been primed with the live mouse, the snake will often readily accept suitably warmed prekills.

2. A second method is to offer your snake a freshly killed mouse. If the snake shows any interest, but seems reluctant to actually accept the mouse, twitch the mouse gently with your fingers or forceps. Move slowly. You must not frighten the snake. The snake will often respond by grasping, constricting, and consuming the mouse.

3. Some snakes will readily accept freshly killed mice but balk at thawed, once-frozen ones. In these cases you can first allow the snake to grasp and constrict the freshly killed mouse. Then, when the snake releases its grip and begins its search for the head (which they usually do to facilitate swallowing) of the freshly killed mouse, quickly remove the mouse and replace it with a readied thawed mouse. The ruse will often work. Although it may take time to acclimate your snake to thawed, once-frozen mice, the effort may be well worthwhile.

Temperature: This is important when feeding snakes. Snakes that are too cold or too hot may not feed. Keeping snakes at a temperature of 80 to 85°F (27–29°C) seems best. Fluctuating temperatures of as little as 10 degrees can cause gastric disturbances and induce regurgitation. If a snake is cooled and kept cool after it has fed, putrefaction of the food animal in the gut of the snake can occur. This can result in the regurgitation of the prey or, in extreme cases, in the death of the snake.

Maintaining the correct temperature in the snake's cage is important. Several methods of providing the necessary temperature gradient have proven satisfactory. If your collection is large, but all specimens can be kept at the same temperature, a room heater may suffice.

Other methods include the use of heat tapes, heating pads, overhead lighting, or ceramic heating elements. Of all these, the heating tapes seem best. They allow the heating of only one end of the cage, permitting the snake to move about and choose either additional warmth or coolness, as it wishes.

Diet

They will readily eat a variety of foods. Kingsnakes and milksnakes not only are ophiophagous (feed on other snakes including their own species), but they opportunistically feed on birds, mammals, amphibians, other reptiles, and the eggs of birds and reptiles as well. It is important for the hobbyist to realize that most kingsnakes and milksnakes are highly cannibalistic and must be housed separately. Milksnakes and kingsnakes are also resistant to the actions of the venoms of native venomous snake species, and are not loathe to consume these species if hungry.

Mechanism of Feeding

Although different species of snakes kill their prey in different ways, collectively, the milksnakes and kingsnakes are powerful constrictors. Contrary to popular belief, constrictors

Kingsnakes and milksnakes are cannibalistic and must be housed separately or the results could end up looking something like this.

do not crush their prey. Bones are not broken. Rather, the snake grasps and coils around the prey, tightening its grip with every exhalation of the prey. Eventually it becomes impossible for the prey to inhale and the victim suffocates. The demise of the prey animal may be quite rapid or may take up to several minutes. The constricting snake will react to any movement of the prey, no matter how small, and will continually tighten its coils until the animal is dead.

Once the snake is certain that the prey animal is dead, it releases its grip. Using its flickering tongue to derive chemical cues, the snake usually searches out the head of the prey to begin its meal. At the nose (rarely, elsewhere) the swallowing commences, the flexible jaws and backward-directed teeth of the snake draw the prey item inward. Once swallowed, the snake curves its powerful body anterior to the prey and with side-to-side motions literally forces the prey animal backward into the stomach.

The larger the prey item, the longer the swallowing process will take. After the prey is in place in the stomach of the snake, the snake will yawn and stretch its distended jaws back into position.

Controlled Diet

A snake's diet may vary in the wild, but it is a good idea to keep captive specimens on a steady, controlled diet. Again, we emphasize the importance of having a ready supply of suitably sized mice available. Snake keeping can be a rewarding experience, but you may quickly become disheartened if you do not have a constant and reliable source of mice.

Domestic Mice

Domestic mice are preferred. If live mice are used they should be stunned first. Fully functional mice have been known to deliver disfiguring or, more rarely, fatal bites to snakes. There is much to be said for feeding your snakes thawed, once-frozen mice.

Thawing: Before thawing the rodents have no odor, require no care, can be bought in bulk lots, and are easily stored until feeding time. Thaw only as many mice as you need and thaw them as close to feeding time as possible.

The use of a microwave oven to thaw mice is not recommended. Microwaving is apt to cook internal organs (thus reducing their benefit to the snake) and to leave hot spots as well. Additionally, microwaving seems to reduce the integrity of the mouse's skin, creating a prey item that is often refused—even by avid feeders. Instead, mice can be thawed beneath the lamps that illuminate snake cages. Use a simple kitchen timer to remind you that there's a mouse "in process."

Size of Food Offered

The size of the meal offered your snake should be neither too large nor too small. Over- or underfeeding will not be in your snake's best interest. One feeding a week usually suffices, with the number of mice offered at that feeding being adjusted to the needs of the individual snake. A snake's rate of growth is determined both by the overall amount eaten and the respective sizes of the prey items. A snake will probably grow more quickly if the size of its prey rodents increases commensurately with the size of the snake.

A young Apalachicola Lowland kingsnake eats a prekilled pinky mouse.

Gray-banded kingsnakes are immensely variable. This example is from Terlingua, Texas.

This is a broken-striped Apalachicola Lowland kingsnake.

Feeding Response Problems

If one of your snakes does not have a good feeding response or refuses to eat entirely, there are several factors to consider. The environment that you have provided and that you control determines the feeding response or lack of feeding response in your specimens. If the cage is warm, dry, and clean, most kingsnakes and milksnakes will thrive in captivity.

If healthy snakes that have been avidly feeding begin refusing food, perhaps shedding is imminent or, if a female, she may be gravid. If the snake is newly acquired, even if captive bred, perhaps a period of acclimatization is all that's necessary before the snake begins feeding.

Other possible reasons for a snake refusing food would include injury, too low a cage temperature, or insecurity brought on by an unsuitable hiding place. If the snake is a wild-collected specimen, it may have endoparasites or a disease, or just be stressed from collection and transport. Perhaps the time of feeding is wrong, maybe the feed item is wrong, or maybe the snake is just generally out of sorts.

Taking all possibilities into consideration and changing or correcting one or more of them might make the difference between a snake that feeds readily and thrives and a specimen that does only marginally well.

TIP

Whetting the Appetite

Consult your veterinarian about the possible use of an appetite stimulant before resorting to force-feeding.

Tricks of the Trade

Methods of inducing a reluctant snake to feed are often called "tricks of the trade." If you have purchased this book, chances are good that you are seriously interested in your snake and intend to pursue the hobby of herpetoculture. It is also quite likely that you have more than one specimen in your collection. This is good, for having several snakes will enable you to make feeding (and other) comparisons. For instance, if all of your specimens suddenly cease feeding you will need to look at factors that affect your entire collection. If only a single specimen ceases to feed, your search for reasons will need to center on the regimen of husbandry that affects only that snake.

Effects of Temperature and Shedding on Feeding

Let's look more closely at temperature or temperature fluctuation as a cause of feeding response problems. Keep in mind that excessively high temperatures can be as debilitating to your snakes as temperatures that are too low.

If your specimen ceases feeding, stabilize the temperature of the cage to between 84 and 88°F (29–31°C). A temperature that is constant or that varies by only a few degrees is important. If the cage temperature is allowed to vary by more than a few degrees (such as by lowering room temperature at night) it can have an adverse effect on the feeding response of your snakes. Additionally, if your snakes have fed, seriously adverse temperatures can induce regurgitation and may seriously injure your snake.

Shedding: As for shedding, think about the last time your snake shed. Snakes generally do not feed before or during the shedding process. However, once they have completed the shed they are usually very hungry and will be searching for food. This is the best time to check your snake's feeding response.

Alternate Foods

If, after trying every other method of inducing your snake to feed, it still refuses, it is time to consider alternate foods. Some milksnakes and kingsnakes, especially some of the tricolored races, feed predominantly on lizards in the wild. This seems especially true of baby gray-banded kingsnakes and certain of the subspecies of the California mountain kingsnake. It is even more true if your snake is a wild-collected specimen. Before your snake loses too much of its body weight due to refusing to feed, offer it a lizard. A swift or an anole is a good choice. This might be just the thing to induce the snake to break its self-imposed fast.

Wild mice, such as white-footed and deer mice and voles (even house mice, for that matter) smell differently than domestic, cage-raised mice, and your snake can easily tell the difference. Try one of the wild mice on a steadfastly reluctant feeder. Don't move on to the next-mentioned step before exhausting all other avenues.

Force-Feeding

Force-feeding a snake is a traumatic experience, and one that we suggest against except in extreme cases. It is far better that you assure

that the snake is eating voluntarily—even voraciously—*before* you purchase it. Nonfeeders or reluctant feeders should be shunned.

Force-feeding adult snakes is usually an exercise in futility that only delays (it can sometimes actually hasten) the snake's demise.

Refusing Food

Occasionally, a kingsnake or milksnake that you have hatched may refuse food. This is especially so if the prey you offer is not a natural part of the snake's diet. For example, many hatchling gray banded kingnakes will refuse pinky lab mice, but will eagerly accept baby lizards (especially skinks or pinky deer mice). Also ascertain that your cage temperature is optimal and that the snake has access to a hiding area in which it can feel safe. Once it feels secure, a snake will often begin feeding voluntarily, providing the offered prey is suitable.

Starving snakes are far more apt to regurgitate a meal than a snake that is feeding readily. If you decide to force-feed your baby snake, do so before obvious signs of starvation are apparent. Experiment, but force-feeding should always be the last resort.

top left: Louisiana milksnakes are small and brightly colored.

top right: The Jalisco milksnake remains uncommon in the hobby.

middle: Striping is one of the designer patterns now seen in Honduran milksnakes.

bottom: This dark phase of the variable kingsnake is termed the "greeri" phase by hobbyists.

*top left: Black scale tipping darkens
many adult Honduran milksnakes.*

*top right: Sinaloan milksnakes are
spectacular creatures.*

*bottom left: New Mexican milksnakes
are slender and brightly colored.*

*bottom right: A tri-colored juvenile
Honduran milksnake.*

If you are planning to maintain a large collection of snakes, you may wish to consider raising your own rodents. However, there are drawbacks to this approach. Among them are space requirements, odor, initial expense, time required for maintenance, disposal of waste, and last, but not least, the need to house your rodents at optimum temperatures. The pros of breeding your own rodents can be summed up in a single word: "convenience!"

Space Requirements

The floor space required for one breeding colony of mice (1 adult male and 3 or 4 adult females) is roughly 12 by 16 inches (30 × 41 cm), about

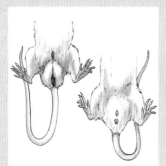

The sexing of mice is important if a breeding colony is to be established. Left indicates a male, and the right illustration a female.

the size of a 5-gallon (19-L) aquarium or a plastic dishpan. Because they are less easily broken, lighter, and their rounded corners make them easier to clean, dishpans are frequently preferred. You may provide water either through the side or from the top, whichever is the most expeditious. If you are using glass-sided aquaria, you may prefer to use one of the watering bottles that hangs inside of the cage.

Watering systems: Watering systems can be either in the form of an individual bottle for each cage or fully automated. Although it takes more work, I prefer the individual bottles over the automated system. Should the contents leak from a bottle the mice will get wet but will survive. If an automated system leaks the mice might drown before the problem is noticed.

Escaping: Since mice are nearly as adept as snakes at escaping their cages, all cages must be 100 percent escape-proof. Consider carefully every aspect of the caging.

Location of colony: Even when kept scrupulously clean, rodent colonies smell. Carefully plan where you will set

up your colony and be certain to incorporate adequate ventilation to the outside into the plans.

Many people keep and breed rodents in their garages, but if the garage is not a detached type, or the rodent colony is not vented to the outside, the unpleasant smell of the colony will eventually invade your household. (If you have ever kept just a few pet mice in your house, you will fully understand the potential for odor.) The odor is much worse during the hotter months of the year; the mice drink much more and their urine output increases.

Temperature

Mice breed best at moderate temperatures. Most show the greatest reproduction at between 65 and 80°F (18–26.7°C). In warm climates, mice can be bred outdoors. Year-round, outdoor breeding of mice is impossible in cold climates. There, having a detached garage would certainly help, but even in such a structure, to realize their fullest breeding potential, the mouse colony would require temperature regulation. If your colony was large, perhaps the cost of insulation, heating, or cooling and providing a water source (as required) could be justified.

Costs

To fully understand the overall costs of breeding rodents, the initial costs of modifying (or constructing) facilities must be considered, as well as the recurring costs of breeding tub and water bottle replacement, bedding, and food. It is helpful and convenient if in the area of your mouse colony, you provide space for the storage of bedding and food. If you have sufficient space for storage, buying these two items in bulk quantities saves both money and trips to a feed store.

Thus, several variables must be considered before setting up a mouse colony. Among others are whether the costs of the materials and the space needed for setting up your colony are sustainable and practical, and whether you have the time to care for the rodents properly once they are set up.

While going to a week-long symposium on herpetoculture (or simply taking a short vacation) will not jeopardize the well-being of your snake collection, not caring for rodents for a couple of days can prove disastrous. Moreover, finding someone capable of providing rodent care in a responsible manner may not always be easy.

If, after reading this section, you are having second thoughts about the practicality of breeding your own rodents, your best bet will be to find a reliable breeder (and a backup source) from whom to purchase your feed mice. Breeding mice is not for everyone!

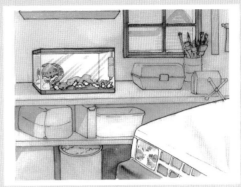

Keeping rodents in a separate room from the snakes reduces odors and will result in a better feeding response of snakes.

More About Wild Mice

There are times when finicky snakes will prove to you that not all rodents—not even all mice—are created equal. Some kingsnakes and milksnakes will steadfastly refuse lab mice as prey but may eagerly accept the young of wild mice (such as deer mice or white-footed mice). Breeders of wild mice occasionally advertise in the classified sections of reptile magazines or online, or may be known to your local pet stores. The disadvantages of wild mice over lab mice are that wild mice often have smaller litters, and, if frightened, a female is more apt than a lab mouse to eat her babies. A note of caution is also necessary here. Wild rodents of many species, including mice, are known vectors of several disease-causing organisms. The possibility is greater in some areas of the United States than in others, but we strongly urge that you not collect mice from the wild. Procure captive-bred wild mice.

REPRODUCTION

*Breeding snakes in captivity
has become popular as both a
hobby and a business. For the
new-breed herpetoculturist it
has become a way of life.*

Captive Breeding

Because of the success of captive breeding, species and subspecies of snakes once considered uncommon are now readily available to all hobbyists. Success with captive breeding has also helped the wild snake populations that were declining from both habitat degradation and collecting pressures exerted by the pet trade.

Besides being a conservation tool of sorts, captive breeding also largely eliminates the presence of parasites and stress related to capture. The babies most commonly offered are already largely, if not entirely, adapted to captivity.

Not all snakes—not even all healthy and seemingly well-adjusted snakes—reproduce readily in captivity. Although in most cases providing a suitable captive environment and regimen of care will eventually result in captive

*Almost translucent at hatching (shown),
adult albino Nelson's milksnakes have
bright, crisp colors.*

breeding success, some snakes are just more easily bred than others. Various milksnakes and kingsnakes, some of which are the most beautifully colored serpents known to science, are among the more easily bred snakes. Even so, numerous factors must be considered before breeding.

Sex Determination

Certainly the most important thing when hoping to breed any but a few parthenogenetic snake species, is to have specimens of both sexes available. Since the members of the genus *Lampropeltis* are not parthenogenetic, accurate sex determination is mandatory.

Tail Shape and Length

Adults may have certain externally visible secondary sexual characteristics. Among these are tail shape and length. The tail of a male snake is heavier, proportionately broader, immediately posterior to the vent, and longer than that of a similarly sized female. The heavier tail base accommodates the inverted, bifurcated, hemipenes. The heavier tail is often more discernable on sexually mature males than on juveniles. In some cases the difference in tail conformation may be minimal, and in all cases it takes much experience to be reasonably sure of the sex.

Probing

The most reliable way to determine the sex of milksnakes and kingsnakes is by probing. A probe is a gently tapered, finely machined, and smooth stainless steel cylinder. Probes are commercially available in a variety of sizes. Probing a snake to determine its sex is a delicate procedure. Using too much force can damage tissue. Hatchlings of the smaller races of milksnake and kingsnake are more difficult to probe safely than larger specimens. Probing newly hatched snakes is not recommended. Probing any snake should be done by a person experienced in the procedure. One safe way to gain experience is by probing road kills.

"Popping"

There is a fairly reliable and safe way of determining the sex of hatchling snakes. The method is called "popping." Gentle pressure is applied with your thumb to the underside of the base of the snake's tail. As you firmly, but gently, roll your thumb upward (toward the snake's vent), if the snake is a male, the pressure will "pop" both tiny hemipenes from their sheaths. If the snake is a female, only two tiny dark dots, one on each side of the vent, will be visible. Although both probing and popping may sound painful, if done properly and gently they are not.

Age

Milksnakes and kingsnakes should not be bred until they are two, or preferably three, years of age. Although sexual maturity can be attained earlier, breeding snakes when they are too young can lead to physical problems. In some species size as well as age should be considered before breeding. Among these species are the larger members of the *getula* complex. These animals should not be bred until they are at least 3 feet (91 cm) long.

Initial breeding of an animal at too early an age or too small a size can not only adversely affect future breeding ability but may result in the female becoming egg bound. There is also the chance that you will lose the eggs, the female, or both. An egg-bound female may often be induced to lay by increasing the cage temperature or by an injection of oxytocin. The latter should be administered only by a qualified individual. If all else fails the eggs may need to be removed by cesarean section. A qualified veterinarian should be consulted.

Preparing Your Female to Breed

Your female needs to be in good health before the winter rest, or brumation period. The most important consideration is that the female be at optimum weight before brumation. If an underweight female is brumated, it is quite likely that she will experience problems if she is bred in the spring. Underweight females produce small eggs, small clutches, or may fail to reproduce altogether. If they do breed and ovulate, underweight females may become debilitated and die during or following egg laying. Feeding an underweight female heavily after her spring emergence from brumation does not necessarily ensure a good clutch of eggs.

Ensuring a Comfortable Brumation (Hibernation)

The term *brumation* refers to a reptile's period of winter dormancy. For mammals, the term is *hibernation*. The minimum recommended duration for reptiles is two months, and three months seems much better. Captive milksnakes and kingsnakes are usually brumated during the colder months of the year. During these days of shortened photoperiod, they would be inactive in the wild as well. During brumation, physiological and hormonal changes occur, readying the reptiles for spring breeding.

Wild specimens carefully choose their hibernacula. Captive specimens are dependent upon us, their keepers, to supply the conditions and temperatures that best suit them. In many areas of the world, a suitable period of brumation can be supplied to captive reptiles by merely reducing the light in a room and simultaneously dropping the room's temperature. The preferred temperature ranges from 48 to 60°F (9–16°C). Drinking water must be kept available.

In subtropical and tropical areas, where average winter temperatures remain well above those needed by brumating snakes, it may be necessary to provide the desired cooling with air conditioning or other artificial means.

Some herpetoculturists prefer to allow natural photoperiods during the winter cooling of their snakes. Both methods seem to work equally well.

TIP

Respiratory Infections

If, during brumation, your snakes develop a respiratory infection or moisture blisters, you should immediately bring them up to 84–88°F (29–31°C) and treat the problem. Ill specimens will seldom survive if left in hibernation.

Although brumation may not be necessary to produce the hormonal changes that bring about ovulation, spermatogenesis, and pheromone production, it does enhance the probability of breeding success.

Post–Brumation Behavior

When you bring your specimens out of their winter dormancy, check all health aspects thoroughly. Any health problems found must be addressed immediately so the animals can still breed. Your potential breeders can now be returned to normal temperatures and offered food after about three days.

Feeding

Some specimens may require a slightly longer period of readjustment and may not feed for a week or 10 days. If specimens are reluctant to feed try offering a smaller than usual prey item in an effort to encourage a feeding response.

Although it may be necessary to offer food frequently to induce some snakes to feed, most post-brumation snakes will have a hearty

Three color phases of the variable kingsnakes are shown here for contrast: orange Nuevo Leon phases (top); tan Nuevo Leon phase (middle), and milksnake phase (bottom).

A blotched phase Apalachicola Lowland kingsnake hatchling.

A scarlet kingsnake emerges from its egg.

appetite. At this time you should strive to increase the body weight of your breeders, feeding them twice rather than once weekly. When hungry your specimens will appear restless. Feeding needs and responses vary according to the specimen. This is not the time of year to get caught with an inadequate food supply.

Shed Cycle

From a few days to a few weeks postbrumation, the snakes will enter a shed cycle. It is at this time when most pheromones are produced and ovulation begins. Immediately following the completed shed cycle, the female

snakes should be introduced to the cages of their prospective mates. It is at this time that ovarian follicles are developing and the females are the most receptive to breeding. Delaying the introduction of the snakes to their mates by only a few days may mean missing a full year's breeding.

Ovarian Follicles

Although it is not necessary to do so, you can feel the developing ovarian follicles of the female snake at this time by gently depressing and running your fingers along the ventral scales from mid-body to the tail.

Breeding Data Chart

Subspecies	Breeding to Egg Laying	Clutch Size	Average	Incubation Time
Gray-Banded Kingsnake (L. alterna)	30 to 60 days	5 to 14	8	60 to 70 days
Prairie Kingsnake (L. c. calligaster)	43 to 55 days	5 to 16	11	54 to 82 days
Variable Kingsnake (L. mexicana)	24 to 46	9 to 15	12	54 to 82 days
Sonora Mountain Kingsnakes (L. pyromelana)	32 to 59	1 to 9	6	58 to 68 days
Queretaro Kingsnake (L. ruthveni)	32 to 46	6 to 10	8	57 to 66 days
California Mountain Kingsnakes (L. zonata)	34 to 56	3 to 8	4	48 to 56 days
Louisiana Milksnake (L.t. amaura)	36 to 48	5 to 9	7	38 to 56 days
Andean Milksnake (L.t. andesiana)	39 to 48	6 to 8	7	72 to 90 days
Mexican Milksnake (L.t. annulata)	28 to 63	2 to 12	7	54 to 73 days
Central Plains Milksnake (L.t. gentilis)	36 to 48	5 to 24	9	48 to 64 days
Pueblan Milksnake (L.t. campbelli)	26 to 54	6 to 12	7	63 to 74 days
Honduran Milksnake (L.t. hondurensis)	22 to 49	2 to 10	6	54 to 72 days
Nelson's Milksnake (L.t. nelsoni)	48 to 64	3 to 10	6	54 to 65 days
Sinaloan Milksnake (L.t. sinaloae)	26 to 49	4 to 16	9	58 to 76 days
Red Milksnake (L.t. syspilia)	39 to 52	6 to 12	8	44 to 62 days
South Florida Kingsnake (L.g. "brooksi")	42 to 60	10 to 20	17	48 to 65 days
California Kingsnake (L.g. californiae)	42 to 63	6 to 23	9	42 to 63 days
Florida Kingsnake (L.g. floridana)	42 to 58	7 to 11	9	44 to 63 days
Eastern Kingsnake (L.g. getula)	44 to 58	5 to 24	11	46 to 64 days
Blotched Kingsnake (L.g. "goini")	42 to 56	10 to 20	17	48 to 65 days
Speckled Kingsnake (L.g. holbrooki)	42 to 64	6 to 22	9	42 to 62 days
Black Kingsnake (L.g. nigra)	44 to 62	6 to 24	12	44 to 62 days
Mexican Black Kingsnake (L.g. nigrita)	42 to 60	6 to 12	8	42 to 60 days
Desert Kingsnake (L.g. splendida)	42 to 64	6 to 12	8	48 to 64 days

Mating

When the male and female are placed together, if she is receptive copulation will occur. The male will trail the female around the cage in an attempt to position and breed her. He may actually grasp her head in his mouth while copulation is occurring.

Gravid (Pregnant) Females

The Breeding Data Chart (page 46) has been compiled from a combination of personal experience, correspondence, and available literature. All data are averages and may vary according to temperature fluctuations and other variables.

Now, assuming your female milksnakes and kingsnakes are gravid—the reptilian equivalent of pregnant—let's continue.

✔ As mentioned in the section on record keeping, you should now have marked the cages of your female snakes with the dates and by which males they were bred.

✔ By checking the Breeding Data Chart, you can estimate when your females should lay their eggs. About 10 days (another variable figure) before deposition your females will complete another skin shedding sequence. This is called the "pre-laying" shed.

✔ Within a few days following the completion of the pre-laying shed, remove the females' water dishes. From this point on the females should be given water only while you are watching them. This will prevent them from laying their eggs in the water dish, something they occasionally do that will kill the embryos.

Note: If you have bred a female to more than one male, use the date of the first breeding as the estimated deposition date. Although some herpetoculturists prefer to breed each female more than once, it takes only a single breeding by a viable male to impregnate the snake. If you are unsure of the virility of a male, breeding the female to a second male is recommended.

Nesting or Egg Deposition Box

The next step is to place a nesting box inside of the female's cage. The nesting box must be large enough for the female to enter and exit easily. The nesting box should be introduced shortly following the female's pre-laying shed. This will allow her to become familiar with the nesting box. Nesting boxes can be as simple as a plastic shoe box half filled with moist (not wet!) sphagnum moss or moist vermiculite. Sphagnum is preferable. Some breeders prefer to leave the lid off of the nesting box; others leave the lid in place but cut a fair-sized access hole in it. The nesting medium will hold its moisture content better when the top is used. Daily checks to determine moisture content and whether the female is using the box are important.

Removing the Eggs

As the deposition date nears, more frequent checks are suggested. At this point, you should be ready to remove the eggs from the female's cage as soon after laying as possible. This prevents the female from crushing, otherwise damaging, or even eating her eggs. Prior to removing the nesting box, visually check the female to ascertain that she has laid all of her eggs.

A covered glass gallon jar, a covered shoe box, or a similar container with an inch or two of moistened vermiculite (one part water to

A striped aberrant California kingsnake.

This Nuevo Leon phase variable kingsnake is devoid of most black pigment.

Anerythristic Florida kingsnakes lack red pigment.

These normal and hypo Florida kingsnakes are siblings.

This San Diego mountain kingsnake is just entering its skin-shedding cycle.

T I P

Incubation Jar or Chamber

Most herpetoculturists prefer to remove the eggs from the nesting box to an incubation jar or chamber. If you do this, have it ready well in advance of the proposed deposition date. Some females may lay their eggs several days earlier than expected, and getting the eggs set up immediately is imperative.

ten parts vermiculite by weight is adequate) or moistened sphagnum moss will suffice. Do not put air holes in the incubation chamber. This will allow moisture evaporation and a lessening of the relative humidity.

Off-the-Wall Incubator

A "completely off-the-wall incubator" achieves excellent results: The materials necessary for this consist of a wide-mouthed gallon jar, its cover, and the cut-off foot part of a discarded pair of panty hose.

✔ Place an inch or two (2–5 cm) of water in the bottom of the gallon (4 L) jar.

✔ Stretch the panty hose over the mouth of the jar so that the foot part is hanging down in the jar.

✔ Place the egg in the toe of the panty hose, which should be suspended an inch or two above the level of the water.

✔ Screw the top of the jar back on so that it holds the egg-laden panty hose securely in place. This creates an incubation chamber with 100 percent relative humidity.

✔ Place the jar in a suitably warm area, ignore for a few weeks, and remove the baby snakes when they hatch.

The incubation substrate must be damp, but not wet, or fungus will appear and the eggs will rot. Check humidity and substrate moisture content on a weekly basis. If it is necessary to remoisten the incubation medium, do so with the mist from a spray bottle. Moisten only the substrate—do not spray the eggs.

Incubation Period

It is imperative to set the eggs up in the incubator box exactly as they are laid. Do not turn or rotate the eggs on their axis. If the eggs are adhering to one another, do not try to separate them. Place them in the incubator box exactly as they are. Occasionally each of the eggs from a clutch may be fully separate from one another. When you move them to an incubator, it is all right if they come in contact with each other, but do not rotate them on their axis.

Once the egg clutch is set up, leave it alone except to make a weekly check.

Temperature: Temperature will partially determine the length of time that the eggs must incubate. A warmer temperature will lessen the time by a few days; cooler temperatures will extend it. Extremes in either direction will kill the embryos.

An elaborate setup or an expensive device is not necessary to hatch snake eggs. Snakes have been reproducing in the wild for millions of years, at times under quite adverse conditions.

In the incubator, snake eggs may be half covered with the moist vermiculite or completely concealed in the moist sphagnum. Seal the container, opening it only for the weekly moisture and egg checks. This weekly inspection will also allow sufficient air circulation and proper oxygen supply. Again, the eggs should not be disturbed in any manner once they are set up. If spoiled eggs can be removed without disturbing the remainder of the clutch, do so. However, if the spoiled egg is a part of a cluster, do not disturb it. The good eggs will hatch regardless of the spoiled ones.

Hatching

As the embryos develop inside the egg, they will derive the necessary nourishment from the yolk. As it absorbs moisture from the substrate, the egg will actually increase slightly in size. By the time hatching occurs, most of the yolk will have been utilized by the embryo.

At hatching, what remains is quickly utilized as an energy source. An umbilical scar (similar to a navel) will show where the embryo was joined to the food supply.

Egg tooth: While the snake is developing, a tiny, sharp "egg tooth" is growing at the very tip of its upper jaw. This tooth is only temporary and is used by the snake to cut its way out of the eggshell. After emerging from the egg, the egg tooth will drop off.

TIP

Checking the Clutch

A natural curiosity often compels a breeder to check the clutch more frequently once the first egg is slit and the hatchling's head is showing. However, doing this may only disturb the young snakes and prolong the emergence process.

Leaving the egg: The new environment outside the egg is usually tested by the hatching snake making several slits in the eggshell. The young snake may poke its head in and out several times, emerging a little more each time until it finally leaves the egg. The hatching process make take several days. Hatchling snakes may sometimes even climb back inside the empty shell to hide.

Setting Up Each Neonate

As soon as the eggs have hatched, each neonate needs to be set up in its own separate container, with a water bowl and hiding area. Paper towels are a good substrate at this point. In about a week the first shed usually occurs, following which the first meal should be offered.

CARING FOR A SICK SNAKE

Since snakes do not usually require daily attention, they are generally thought of as fairly low-maintenance animals. However, if snakes are not kept clean, warm, and dry, problems that can result in a costly veterinarian bill (or even the snake's death) may arise.

Quarantine Period

When you acquire a new specimen a period of quarantine is most important. This will help prevent the spread of disease to any other specimens in your collection. A 90-day quarantine period should be sufficient to determine the overall health of the specimen. Undue stress decreases a snake's ability to ward off infection and will enable a disease to debilitate a snake at a much quicker rate. This is especially true of juveniles. Any newly acquired specimens should be checked for parasites, strength, alertness, and symptoms of respiratory distress. All specimens, but especially those from the neotropics, should have a routine fecal exam done by a qualified veterinarian.

A tangerine Honduran milksnake.

Cage Cleaning

Simple routine cage cleaning eliminates both bacteria and fungus that may be present. Both cage and substrate should be dry. Commercially available disinfectants, such as Rocal and Nolvasan, are excellent but expensive. A most efficacious and inexpensive sterilizing solution can be made by mixing one quarter cup of liquid chlorine bleach with 1 or 2 teaspoonfuls of dishwashing liquid and one gallon (3.8 L) of water. After sterilizing, be sure to rinse well and let dry.

Between complete cage cleanings, all fecal material and areas of wet substrate should be removed as quickly as possible. By so doing you will prevent the growth of fungi and bacteria. Poorly ventilated cages are prone to buildups of odor and moisture. Should this occur install additional ventilation panels.

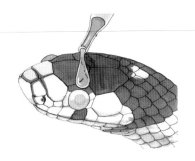

Water

Water should be kept fresh and clean at all times. Water that is not changed on a regular basis can transmit parasites or bacteria. Changing water twice weekly should be sufficient and disinfecting the water bowls twice monthly will eliminate the potential for problems. Of course, if a snake makes stools in its water, the bowl should be removed, cleaned, refilled, and replaced right away.

Shedding

The outer keratinous layer of the epidermis of a snake does not grow with the animal; it is shed periodically. The shedding sequence is more frequent in snakes that are growing rapidly, and may then occur several times a

Check the shedded skin to make sure the skin over the eyes has completely shed. If not, a drop of mineral oil is helpful in removing the "eye" cap.

year. Older snakes, which grow more slowly, shed their skin less frequently. Most snakes from temperate climates shed their skin soon after emerging from hibernation; and if a female, may shed again prior to oviposition or, if of a live-bearing form, the birth of her young. One or more shedding sequences can also be triggered by disease or injury.

Preecdysis and Ecdysis

The act of preparing to shed is called *preecdysis;* the act of shedding is called *ecdysis.* As a snake prepares to shed its skin it often seeks areas of seclusion. The old skin begins to separate from the new that has formed beneath it. As the cleavage between the two increases, the colors and patterns of the snake and its vision become obscured. The snake takes on a milky, opaque appearance. This stage is often referred to by hobbyists as "blue" or "opaque." At this time the snake will be at its most irritable, often resisting handling and refusing to feed.

The snake will often seek a darkened, moist area in which to coil. Some keepers place a receptacle of moistened sphagnum in the cage at this time. It may even immerse itself in its water bowl. A day or two prior to the actual shedding, the appearance of opacity will diminish. By this time the cleavage between the skins will have loosened the old skin from the lips. By rubbing against a roughened sur-

To help a snake shed its skin force the snake to soak in tepid water.

face the snake will work the old skin completely free from its jaws and begin to work its way forward, crawling out of the inverting old skin, the way you would peel off a tight glove or sock.

Helping Your Snake Shed Its Skin

Eyecaps

Captive snakes may occasionally have problems shedding their skin. It is important to check the shed to ascertain that the eyecaps (the brilles or spectacles) have completely shed. These will have the appearance of mini-contact lenses in the old skin. Failure of the eyecaps to shed can cause permanent eye damage or even blindness.

If the eyecaps have not been shed, either force your snake to soak in tepid water to loosen the caps or place a drop of mineral oil onto the cap to moisten and loosen it. Then, carefully grasping a corner of the eyecap, gently lift the cap free. Use extreme care when doing this. You must not injure the eye itself. If you do not feel confident enough to do this yourself, seek assistance from someone who is more experienced.

Tail and Patches

Also check the tail of the snake to ensure that no shed remains on the tip. Nor should patches remain on the body. If it does remain, the drying old skin can lead to infection or

How to help the snake shed its skin: grip the leading edge of the skin patch with tweezers and gently peel backward toward the tail.

TIP

Cage Humidity
The most common reason for an incomplete shed is insufficient cage humidity. High relative humidity and the presence of a soaking bowl (or receptacle of moistened sphagnum) is particularly important at this time.

death of the tissue beneath it. If the snake does not shed its entire skin from nose to tail in one complete piece, this could (but not always) indicate a problem with either the health of the snake or, more often, with its cage conditions.

If your snake does retain patches of skin it is important that they be removed.
✔ The first step is to soften the skin and loosen its area of adhesion by allowing (or forcing, if necessary) the snake to soak in a receptacle containing an inch or two (2–5 cm) of tepid water, or moistened sphagnum, or paper towels.

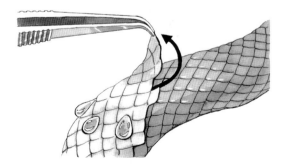

This is a blotched-phase adult Apalachicola Lowland kingsnake.

Despite beliefs to the contrary, eastern kingsnakes have variable patterns and colors.
This broad-banded adult is from an area near Charleston, South Carolina.

top: Bubblegum
Honduran milksnakes
are pink and white.

middle: The scarlet
kingsnake is the most
divergent member of
the milksnake group.

A banded aberrant
California kingsnake.

✔ Once this is done, grip the leading edge of the skin patch with your fingers or tweezers and peel it gently backward. If the snake has soaked long enough, removing the skin patches should be an easy matter.

✔ If it is the tail tip skin that has remained, grasp the tail gently between thumb and forefinger or with a warm, dampened washcloth and, moving from front to rear, gently peel the skin backward.

✔ Adequate relative humidity and the presence of a branch or a rock during the shedding process usually permits the snake to shed with no help from you.

Endoparasites (Internal Parasites)

Internal parasites may cause a snake to exhibit certain signs of abnormal behavior. Periodic fecal exams can detect the presence of these endoparasites before the snake has reached a point where treatment may be futile. Fecal exams should be routinely performed on newly acquired, wild-collected milksnakes and kingsnakes. Because of a preponderance of endoparasites in snake habitats, these exams become even more important if the new specimen is from the neotropics.

Signs: Some obvious signs of parasitism are refusal to feed, regurgitation, rapid weight loss, inactivity, and frequent gaping. Any unusual stool conditions, such as diarrhea, mucous, blood, or discoloration, may indicate internal parasites. Any time there is a question, a fresh fecal sample should be examined by a competent individual.

Veterinarians usually have the experience and equipment to make proper diagnoses. Veterinarians who are reptile specialists can also prescribe the correct medication and dosages to ensure the snake's health.

Cestodes

Better known as tapeworms, cestodes are common endoparasites that can be picked up when the snake ingests a food source that is a host of the worm. The presence of these segmented worms is not always easily diagnosed and they are often not detected until the infestation is quite large. The presence of large numbers of these worms can cause inflammation and bowel obstruction, and lead to eventual malnutrition of the snake.

When passed in the snake's stools, tapeworm segments can actually be seen by the naked eye. However, it may be better to have occasional fecal exams performed by a qualified technician. If cestodes are present, they can be eradicated by the use of Droncit (praziquantel). The dosage of 5 mg/kg should be administered by intramuscular injection. A second injection should be given two weeks later.

Trematodes

Trematodes, another internal parasite, are more commonly called flukes. They have been seen in the snake's mouth as well as its kidneys, intestines, lungs, and esophagus. They are common in *Lampropeltis*, and are acquired when the snake eats a food item that is a carrier. If present in large numbers in the respiratory system or mouth of the snake, the snake may gape frequently. Flukes seen in the mouth of the snake may be removed with a cotton swab. Those present internally can be eradicated by an intramuscular injection of Droncit (praziquantel) at a dose of 5–8 mg/kg. Feeding prefrozen thawed out rodents effectively eliminates the possibility of trematode infestation.

Nematodes

Reptiles are hosts to literally hundreds of types of nematodes, or roundworms. They normally occur in the stomach and intestines. Roundworms of the genus *Polydelphis* are common and may be transmitted to your snake when it eats infected lizards or rodents. Although not immediately fatal, roundworms should be eradicated as soon as they are detected.

Roundworms can not only cause malnutrition in a snake but can also give rise to secondary bacterial infection. Although roundworms can be easily seen with the naked eye, periodic fecal exams will alert you to their presence more quickly. Panacur (fenbendazole) administered orally at a dosage of 25 mg/kg every two weeks for two to three applications is the recommended treatment.

Although there are other varieties of worms that infest reptiles in general, most are not commonly found in milksnakes and kingsnakes.

However, the prey items of the snakes may be intermediate hosts. Any signs or symptoms should be checked out by a qualified veterinarian. Periodic fecal exams are strongly recommended.

Protozoans

Besides the more obvious worms and flukes, numerous other internal parasites may be encountered in snakes.

• One of the more prevalent ones is the protozoan, *Endamoeba invadens*. This invasive scourge attacks the liver, and small and large intestines, and is carried through the lymphatic and circulatory systems. Amoeba can cause ulcerations and necrosis. Signs are variable and may include mucous, blood, or bile in the stools. If untreated, amoeba infestations can lead to anorexia, dehydration, and death of the snake. The drug of choice is Flagyl (metronidazole). The dosage may vary from 25 to 50 mg/kg. This is administered orally every two weeks until fecal exams are negative.

• Coccidia of the genera *Caryospora, Cryptosporidium, Eimeria,* or *Isopora* may also occur in your snakes. Fecally contaminated food, water, or substrate can cause and spread protozoan infestations. Scrupulously clean cages will prevent the spread. Signs include mild diarrhea, dehydration, and anorexia. If untreated, these can lead to death. A fresh stool specimen is needed for a diagnosis. Two three-day treatments of Albon (sulfadimethoxine) with a break of three days between should correct the problem. Albon is administered orally. The initial suggested dosage is 90 mg/kg. The following two of the three treatments will be administered at dosages of 45 mg/kg.

The Blair's phase of the gray-banded kingsnake was once considered a full species.

A high-white aberrant California kingsnake.

A portrait of a scarlet kingsnake.

right top: The muted phase of the Pueblan milksnake is called the apricot phase by hobbyists.

right middle: This color phase is referred to as the red tangerine albino Honduran milksnake.

right bottom: Ghost Honduran milksnakes lack black scale tipping.

Adult black milksnakes lack most contrasting colors.

Flagellates

There are several species of flagellates that may be encountered. Although these occur most commonly in tropical American sub-species of milksnakes, flagellates have also been reported in North American members of the genus. Blood or mucous in the stools or diarrhea may indicate the presence of flagellates. Failure to treat leads to anorexia and subsequent debilitation in snakes. A direct fecal smear is needed for a correct diagnosis. Normal treatment for flagellates is Flagyl (metronidazole) administered orally at 25–50 mg/kg once biweekly until fecal smears are negative.

Ectoparasites (External Parasites)

Since the advent of the hobby, snake mites, *Ophionyssus,* have plagued collections and distressed hobbyists. Mites feed on the blood of reptiles. The heat and humidity of a terrarium provides an ideal environment for the proliferation of snake mites. Mites, although minute, are easily visible. They can be seen moving about the cage and over the body of a captive snake.

Mites

When feeding, mites attach themselves to the snake in areas where the skin is easily penetrated by their proboscis. Such places as interstitial areas (between scales) and in the vent, nostrils, and eye sockets are favored by mites.

A snake plagued with a mite infestation shows obvious signs of discomfort. The snake will move nearly continually (often with abnormally jerky motions), rub its face and body along the sides of the cage or the cage furniture, and if coiled, twitch and frequently change positions. Infestations of snake mites also causes shedding, as this is one way snakes rid themselves of mites in the wild. If you see frequent, repeated shedding, check your snakes closely for mites.

Hiding places: Cracks and crannies in cages and decorated terraria provide ideal hiding places for nonfeeding mites. For this reason, the easily cleaned and sterilized plastic containers with rounded corners and no lips are strongly recommended for large or perpetually changing collections. If uncontrolled, mites will spread, distressing and debilitating entire collections.

Removing mites: Mites can be removed from snakes by soaking the snakes in tepid water and removing those from the nonsubmerged areas (nose and top of head) with a cotton swab.

Cleaning the cage: Before placing the snake back in its cage, the cage must be cleaned and de-mited.

✔ Remove all substrate and mist the entire interior of the cage with a warm 5 percent solution chlorine bleach and soapy water. Do not use phenol-based disinfectants. Take particular pains to clean any areas of overhanging frame or other such areas of seclusion.

✔ Rinse the cage thoroughly after cleaning it.

✔ Dry the cage (a hair drier works ideally for this purpose), add clean substrate and sterilized cage furniture.

✔ Before placing your snake back in its completely cleaned cage, again check the snake for mites. If any are seen, remove them immediately.

✔ Replace the snake in its cage and keep careful watch on both snake and cage for 10 days.

Severe mite infestations: Vapona No-Pest Strips or their equivalents also effectively combat mite problems. When using these, it is necessary to ventilate the cage, remove the snake's water dish, and be certain the snake cannot come in direct contact with the insecticide-impregnated strip. Merely hanging a strip in a room and expecting it to eradicate mites in all of the cages simultaneously is not realistic. Each cage needs to be treated separately. A section of strip about one-quarter inch by 1 inch (6–25 mm) in size will effectively treat a 20-gallon (76-L) (12 × 12 × 24 inches [30 × 30 × 61 cm]) terrarium or cage.

To eradicate a severe mite infestation the section of No-Pest Strip should be placed in the cage and left for three days. The insecticide in the strip kills only the mites themselves, not their eggs. Repeat the entire process in nine days to kill the newly hatched mites. Setting the section on top of the cage for two to three hours twice weekly may work as a prophylaxis but will probably not quickly eradicate a severe infestation of mites. Even when using Vapona it is a good idea to thoroughly clean the snake's cage and cage furniture. Replace old bedding with new.

Trichlorfon spray may also be used for combatting snake mites. Use the normal amount that is indicated for cattle (directions are on bottle). First, remove and thoroughly wash the water bowl. Make a 0.16 percent solution of the Trichlorfon by using 2 teaspoonfuls of the standard solution and adding this to just less than a pint of water. Best results are obtained by using a spray bottle and lightly spraying the snake and the cage. Let the cage air out until dry and then place the snake back in the cage.

Do not put the water bowl back in the cage for 24 hours, allowing all traces of the Trichlorfon to dissipate from the cage. After 24 hours has elapsed it is safe to refill and replace the water bowl.

Repeat the Trichlorfon treatment in two weeks. The treatment should retain its effectiveness for about a month.

Ticks

Ticks are not normally a problem with kingsnakes and milksnakes. Even when present, as on newly collected wild snake specimens, there are seldom more than one or two, or in extreme cases a half dozen, on a snake. Should ticks be present you may remove them by grasping their body with forceps or tweezers and pulling them gently off the snake.

Before trying to remove ticks, relax them by daubing their bodies with alcohol. Apply even pressure; do not jerk them when freeing them. The tick must come away from the snake intact. After removal the tick site should be cleaned with either hydrogen peroxide or a Povidine solution. Finally, apply an antibiotic ointment such as Neosporin to prevent infection.

Mouth Rot

Mouth rot, known also as infectious stomatitis and ulcerative gingivitis, is a serious and all too common problem among captive snakes. Early signs are an abundance of oral mucus. Next, a cheesy (caseous) substance forms on and around the gums and teeth. Hydrogen peroxide or a Povidine solution may cure the problem if it is caught in its earliest stages. The snake's mouth must be swabbed out daily. Adding a triple sulfa solution (one ounce per gallon [24 g/4 L]) to the drinking water is also helpful.

Note: Antibiotics are available for this type of infection, but it is best to have sensitivity tests performed by a qualified veterinarian before using such a regimen of medication.

SPECIES/SUBSPECIES ACCOUNTS

Striking patterns and coloration have made members of the genus **Lampropeltis,** *kingsnakes and milksnakes, eagerly sought by private collectors. Today, even kingsnakes and milksnakes of what were once considered uncommon subspecies are readily available. This fact and the ease with which they may be maintained, fed, and handled draw many enthusiasts to these snakes.*

Prairie and Mole Kingsnakes

Lampropeltis calligaster
(Harlan, 1827)

This is a complex of three subspecies. Although all are secretive, two—the prairie and the mole kingsnake—are well known, but much about the life and distribution of the South Florida mole kingsnake remains conjectural. It is mostly males, probably searching for receptive females with which to breed, that are found prowling above ground.

Size: At a substantiated length of 56 inches (142 cm), the prairie king is the largest of the three. The mole kingsnake attains a length of 48 inches (122 cm), and the greatest length the

Although variable in color intensity, most pale milksnakes are aptly named.

South Florida mole kingsnake is known to attain is 34 inches (88 cm).

Color: Both the prairie kingsnake and the mole kingsnake are known to be variable in color, but only a single color phase of the South Florida mole king has been seen. Hatchlings and juveniles are quite like the adults in appearance but may be a bit more brightly colored.

These are rather even-dispositioned snakes and, despite not being brightly colored, are widely kept by hobbyists.

Prairie Kingsnake

Lampropeltis calligaster calligaster
(Harlan, 1827)

Color: Prairie kingsnakes occur in both a dark and light phase, as well as in many intermediate colors between. They have about 60 dark dorsal blotches against a lighter ground coloration. The blotches tend to have straight or concave leading and trailing edges. Lateral spots are present, and often are numerous and well defined. Ground color ranges from light tan to dark-olive and the dark-edged blotches may vary from red to dark olive. Individuals with stripes rather than blotches and albinos have been collected and are established in captivity.

Habitat: Favored habitats include open fields and prairies as well as lightly wooded areas of the Midwest.

One, a dark phase individual recently found in Missouri, was tightly secreted beneath a fallen side to a weathered and rotted shed. Even when it was disturbed to take a photograph, it made no attempt to bite or move.

Eggs: The egg clutch of the prairie kingsnake averages 11 eggs per clutch.

The similar-appearing Great Plains rat snake is often mistaken for a prairie kingsnake but has a divided anal plate.

Range: The range of the prairie kingsnake is from Indiana west to Nebraska through the Mississippi Valley to eastern Texas and western Louisiana.

Mole Kingsnake
Lampropeltis c. rhombomaculata
(Holbrook, 1940)

Because it is so secretive, the presence of this snake may go undetected, even where it is fairly common. Babies and juveniles are strongly patterned, but old adults may be almost unicolored.

Color: The dorsal blotch color varies from reddish to dark olive-green. The body color of this variable and slender snake may be pale tan when young but darken to a dark olive-brown (or nearly black) in old adults. The ground color of

occasional examples is pale red. Vestiges of stripes may develop with age. Albinos have been wild collected and are occasionally captive bred. The well-defined and well-separated dorsal blotches usually number 56 or fewer. The anterior and posterior edges of the spots are usually straight to slightly convex. Lateral spotting may be profuse or virtually absent.

Size: Adults average 3 feet (88 cm).

Range: The mole king is seldom surface-active except after heavy rains or when it is dug up or found under surface debris. It is a species of both cultivated fields and woodlands from Maryland southward to northern Florida and westward to Tennessee and northeastern Louisiana. The southern limits of the range are not well defined.

Mole kings are not as commonly bred in captivity as the prairie king.

South Florida Mole Kingsnake
Lampropeltis c. occipitolineata
(Price, 1987)

Color: This, the smallest race in this group, is still known from comparatively few specimens. From 75 to 80 dorsal blotches seem the norm. Since the largest specimens yet found have had prominent, contrasting patterns, it is surmised that the color and pattern of this southernmost race of mole kingsnake do not darken or obscure with age.

Only a few specimens have yet been bred in captivity.

Range: The range of this remains imperfectly delineated. Specimens have been collected in Brevard, Highlands, DeSoto, and Okeechobee counties, Florida. Most specimens found have been males, discovered in the spring of the year as they cross dirt roads at night. This snake occurs both in agriculture and open prairieland as well as in areas covered with sparse second growth.

Common Kingsnakes

Lampropeltis getula
(Linnaeus, 1776)

In this complex of seven recognized subspecies (and a number of problematic forms, some of which are considered subspecies by some authorities) are the largest of the kingsnakes.

Size: The eastern kingsnake has been verified as attaining 85 inches (26 m) in total length and has a considerable girth.

Range: As a species this snake occurs from the Atlantic to the Pacific, and from New Jersey in the east and Oregon in the west to the southern tip of Baja, central Mexico, and the tip of the Florida Peninsula. These snakes inhabit areas as diverse as swamps, prairies, and deserts and occupy areas from sea level elevation to altitudes of nearly 7,000 feet (2,134 m) in the mountains.

Color: The ground color of all is dark, and patterns, which may be in the form of bands, rings, chains, or speckles, are light. The kingsnakes with the lightest color occur in southern Florida.

Common Kingsnakes, Eastern and Central Races

Eastern Kingsnake

Lampropeltis getula getula
(Linnaeus, 1766)

Color: In the north this is a shiny, jet black snake with a pattern of narrow, chalk white, chainlike markings. More southernly examples may be browner and have wider bands but the scales are equally shiny. Because of its markings,

it is often referred to as a "chain kingsnake." Hatchlings have a varying amount of red on the flanks. This usually fades quickly as the snake grows.

Range: Although it may be found far from water, the eastern kingsnake is most common near the sunny edges of levees, marshes, canals, and ponds. The range of the eastern kingsnake is from New Jersey and West Virginia to northern Florida.

This is a very popular snake with hobbyists. Albinos and those with lavender ground color have now been genetically engineered.

Some examples are placid and will allow themselves to be indiscriminately handled while others may strike furiously if disturbed.

On warm mornings these snakes bask amid grasses and vines or in rock rubble but retreat into the burrows of rodents or beneath debris when summer temperatures dry the grasses and the topsoil.

Eggs: Up to a dozen eggs are laid in a clutch. Well-fed captives may produce two clutches a year.

Florida Kingsnake

Lampropeltis g. floridana (formerly *L. g. brooksi*)
(Barbour, 1919)

Size and color: This big (to 69 inches [175 cm]), light-colored kingsnake can be encountered from about the latitude of southern Lake Okeechobee, Florida, to the tip of the peninsula. Each of the dark scales contains a light spot and the crossbands are narrow and most visible dorsally. Light lateral blotches are present but may be very diffuse, hence not easily visible. Examples from areas of light substrate (such as the oolitic limestone edged canals and limestone prairies) can be particularly light in color while those

The South Florida mole kingsnake is still considered a rarity.

from the mucklands are noticeably darker. Males may be lighter and larger than the females. Hatchlings have much darker saddles than the adults. The saddles usually contain russet or mahogany suffusions, but in most cases this color is lost quickly as the snake grows.

These snakes are becoming increasingly difficult to find in the wild as the cities in south Florida continue to grow and usurp habitat. It would seem that the pure phenotype is now also difficult to find in herpetoculture. Instead, hobbyists have genetically engineered albinos (lacking black), flames (retain red coloration), lavenders (white with a purplish tinge), snows (lacking red and black pigment), white-sided (self-explanatory), and anerythristics (lacking red). Today, even when a captive-bred Florida kingsnake with classic coloration is seen, aberrant genes are usually present but masked.

Eggs: A clutch can contain up to 12 eggs.

Range: These light yellow and olive-tan kingsnakes were never actually restricted to the extreme southern peninsula as many thought. They are actually found from the vicinity of Tampa Bay southward along the Gulf Coast to Card Sound, but it was there, amid the Manchineel and buttonbush, that they were the best known and most abundant.

Peninsula Intergrade Kingsnake

Lampropeltis g. getula x *L. g. floridana*
(Blanchard, 1919)

Color: This is a widespread and very abundant kingsnake. This brown and cream kingsnake with a very busy pattern was long referred to (in error) as the Florida kingsnake. Hatchlings have patches of raspberry red along the sides, but this color quickly fades as the snakes grow.

Habitat: Today, these snakes are found in the sod and sugarcane fields. This common kingsnake occurs along irrigation canals, where prey items such as frogs and water snakes are abundant. They may also be found beneath surface debris, near jumbles of oolitic limestone, and amid profuse growths of recumbent blackberries and other vines.

Range: They occur along much the length of the Florida Peninsula from Marion County southward to Miami-Dade County, but are absent from the Gulf Coast.

Size: An adult length of 60 inches (152 cm) is common.

Eggs: A clutch can contain up to 16 eggs.

Apalachicola Lowland Kingsnake

Lampropeltis g. getula x *L. g.* ssp.
(Neill and Allen, 1949)

Range: This beautiful and variable kingsnake remains a true taxonomic problem. It is restricted

Prairie kingsnakes are widespread and common.

in distribution to the mixed woodlands of the Apalachicola River Valley of Florida's central panhandle. It would seem that the snake is both rare and secretive. Some authorities have suggested that there are now far many more Apalachicola Lowland kingsnakes in captive breeding programs than are left in the wild. At the periphery of the tiny range of this snake, extensive intergradation with the eastern kingsnake occurs. These intergrade examples are of variable appearance but are usually much darker in coloration than the Apalachicola Lowland king.

Size: The Apalachicola Lowland kingsnake may occasionally attain a length of 74 inches (23 m). It epitomizes color and pattern variability.

Color: Patternless, those possessing broken or complete stripes that are either darker or lighter than the body color, and variably blotched morphs are all well known. It is probable that the patternless speckled form is the closest in appearance to the supposed ancestral stock and that the blotched phase from which the animal was described in 1949 is the most distant in appearance. Body scales each have a light dot. The belly is often predominantly dark. Blotched hatchlings bear a variable suffusion of russet or strawberry on the sides; patternless hatchlings may be entirely suffused with an orangish red. This brilliance may fade fast with growth or be retained for quite some time. The natural variability has made this snake a hobbyist favorite. Breeders have now stabilized a "flame" morph that retains the red coloration throughout life.

Eggs: A clutch contains from 6 to 12 eggs. Blotched, striped, and patternless hatchlings may emerge from the same clutch.

Outer Banks Kingsnake
Lampropeltis g. sticticeps
(Barbour and Engles, 1942)

Size and Range: The subspecific validity of this large (to 72 inches [22 m]) kingsnake is questionable. It is restricted to the vicinity of Cape Hatteras, North Carolina, where it occurs both on barrier islands and the mainland.

Color: The Outer Banks kingsnake is of variable color and pattern intensity. Hatchlings are quite like "normal" eastern kingsnakes in appearance, but usually have a few speckled scales dorsally. Ontogenetic (age related) changes can be pronounced. Some examples develop a white (or yellowish) spot on virtually every dark scale; others have comparatively few. The center of the broad dark saddles may be noticeably lighter than where they abut the light bands. Although examples of normal coloration are well established in captive breeding programs, aberrancies seem yet unreported.

Eggs: A clutch may contain up to 12 eggs.

Speckled Kingsnake

Lampropeltis g. holbrooki
(Stejneger, 1902)

Range: The "salt and pepper kingsnake" is a large and beautiful form with a wide distribution in the eastern-central states. The speckled kingsnake ranges southward from Illinois and Iowa to eastern Texas and southwestern Alabama.

Color: The cross banding is usually not well defined and most dark scales contain a single central light dot. Hobbyists have defined three forms: the Mississippi Valley (lowland) form, which has virtually no crossbands but has vivid spotting; the rather prominently crossbarred and prominently speckled western form, and the eastern form which has indistinct but readily discernible crossbars as well as prominent speckling. Albino speckled kings have been field collected and several albino strains are now well established in collections. Although many hobbyists

do not feel the albinos of this race to be as attractive as those of certain others, albino *holbrooki* are a nice break from the norm and are rather eagerly sought by newcomers to the hobby.

Range and habitat: At the western edge of its range the speckled kingsnake intergrades extensively with the desert king, and along the eastern edge of its range it intergrades with the black king. The habitat of this ubiquitous snake varies widely, encompassing open prairies, grasslands, upland woods, swamps, marshes, and river edges. It utilizes the elevated habitats afforded by dikes and levees extensively.

Size: This is one of the more slender members of the getula complex. Although it has been recorded at lengths of up to 6 feet (2 m), captives have bred at 30 inches (9 m) in length. This form has a reputation for being rather aggressive when disturbed, but most captives become gentle after a short period of time.

Eastern Black Kingsnake

Lampropeltis g. nigra
(Yarrow, 1882)

Color: This is the least colorful of the common kingsnakes of eastern North America. In many respects, *nigra* resembles a dark and poorly patterned speckled kingsnake. Indeed, there is a rather extensive zone of intergradation where the ranges of the two abut and overlap. At the eastern and southern extremes of its range, *nigra* intergrades with the eastern kingsnake. *Nigra* is basically a black snake. The chainlike dorsal crossbars are thin and irregular. Yellow or white specks are often present on some of the ventrolateral scales. This flecking is most prominent at the base of the crossbars. Some specimens may also have vague speckling present dorsally. The upper labials (lip scales) are usually prominently marked with vertical yellow markings. The chin is light; the venter is irregularly checkered.

Habitat: In ideal habitat, this dark, at times irascible, kingsnake may be quite common. Like most kingsnakes, *nigra* prefers the environs of watercourses. It can be present in some numbers near swamps, marshes, and bogs, but also wanders far afield into meadows, pastures, and woodlands. It persists even in areas of human habitation and may be encountered in oil fields, overgrown lots, and fencerows.

The lack of color and rather bad disposition combine to make this one of the least popular of kingsnake races with hobbyists. However, it is hardy, long-lived, and easily cared for.

Size: Occasional specimens of the black kingsnake may exceed 4.5 feet (135 cm) by a few inches. Most are fully grown at 3.5 to 4 feet (104–122 cm) in overall length however.

Range: The black king occurs from southern Ohio and Illinois southward to central Alabama and northwestern Georgia.

Common Kingsnakes, Western Races

California Kingsnake

Lampropeltis g. californiae
(Blainville, 1835)

Color: This is another of the common kingsnake group that varies tremendously in both ground color and pattern. The ground color may be black, brown, or nearly tan, with a pattern of white or cream-colored bands, stripes, or a combination of banding *and* striping. The striped morph seems the most common in the southernmost part of the California kingsnake's range. When talking about "normal" California kingsnakes, hobbyists and field researchers generally think of those specimens that have from 20 to 45 white bands against a deep brown ground color. The light bands widen ventrolaterally. The venter may be banded, dark or light. Other colors and patterns (including the naturally occurring striped phase) are thought to be somewhat abnormal and worthy of mention. Hatchlings bearing stripes, bands, and combinations have emerged from different eggs in the same clutch. In bygone years the striped and banded forms were considered different subspecies. Naturally occurring albinos and "lavenders" are well documented.

The now invalid subspecific names of *boylii* (typically banded kings of California), *yumensis* (desert phase with black ground coloration), *nitida* (striped southern Baja phase), and *conjuncta* (mid-Baja banded phase) are still occasionally applied by hobbyists and breeders.

Probably because of the immense variation provided by its many colors and patterns, the California kingsnake has become the most commonly bred subspecies of the genus. Adding to its pleasing characteristics are a placid disposition and a readiness to feed and reproduce. California kingsnakes of innumerable colors with patterns never seen in the wild have been developed.

Eggs: Eggs most commonly number from 5 to 12 and "double clutching" is not uncommon when the females are healthy and heavy.

Here are a few colors and morphs often offered to hobbyists by breeders: Normal-Banded, Wide-Banded, Banded (50 percent yellow), Mixed Pattern, Ruby-Eyed Albino, Albino Normal-Banded, Albino Wide-Banded, Normal Striped, Albino Striped, Albino Mixed Pattern,

Many speckled kingsnakes will draw their neck into an "S" and strike when disturbed.

Desert Phase, High Yellow (Banana or Crazy), Lavender, and additional combinations continue to appear.

Size: This is one of the smaller races of the common kingsnake. Adults seldom exceed 4 feet (122 cm) in overall length.

Habitat: Although usually diurnal, during the very hottest times of the year the California kingsnake is also active after dark. It is found in habitats as varied as desert lowlands, rolling foothills, and sparsely forested, pine oak-clad, mountains. They are often found beneath surface cover and can be quite common around deserted homesteads, the edges of dumps, and in other such areas where man-made debris is profuse. If in desertlands, California kingsnakes are often closely tied to the environs of natural watercourses and cattle tanks.

Range: The California kingsnake ranges southward from southwestern Oregon to southern Utah, the southern half of Nevada, all but eastern Arizona, all of California, and all of Baja California. The California and the desert kingsnakes intergrade in southcentral Arizona.

Mexican Black Kingsnake
Lampropeltis g. nigrita
(Zweifel and Norris, 1955)

Color: Now a popular kingsnake in collections, adults of the Mexican black kingsnake (do not confuse this with the eastern black kingsnake, *L. g. nigra*) are usually an unrelieved jet black both dorsally and ventrally. An occasional specimen may have a very few flecks of yellow ventrolaterally (and even fewer dorsally). Hatchlings and juveniles may be vaguely crossbarred but become darker with each shed. This race lacks yellow on the upper labials. This is the only one of the common kingsnakes that does not exhibit some type of pattern.

Because of the summer heat in their desert habitat, Mexican black kingsnakes are largely nocturnal.

Size: The adult length of this race is about 3.5 feet (104 cm).

Eggs: A normal clutch consists of 4 to 9 eggs.

Range: Mexican black kingsnakes range from northwestern Sinaloa, Mexico, northward through the state of Sonora to extreme southern Arizona. Most of the specimens in Arizona show signs of intergradation with either California or desert kingsnakes.

Desert Kingsnake
Lampropeltis g. splendida
(Baird and Girard, 1853)

Color: The ground color of this variable race may range from black to brown. The crossbars and speckles are white, cream, or yellow. The number of crossbars (hence the size of the dorsal blotches) is variable. The crossbars may number as few as 42 or as many as 97. The lateral scales are prominently flecked with tan or yellow. Darker examples can be surprisingly bright and pretty. Hatchling and juvenile specimens are very brightly colored but often fade noticeably as adulthood approaches. Some examples have the entire head and anterior neck solid black. Hobbyists refer to these as "sockheads."

Size and habitat: This hardy snake breeds readily and is fairly small. Gravid female desert kings that are barely 3 feet (91 cm) long are often found crossing roadways. During early spring and late fall, desert kings are largely diurnal. As the desert temperatures become warmer, the desert kingsnakes adopt crepuscular and nocturnal patterns of activity. Although adult desert kingsnakes can attain a length of 5 feet (152 cm), most adults are at least a foot (30 cm) shorter. The habitat of the desert kingsnake includes deserts, irrigated fields, and agricultural areas and the environs of streams, rivers, ponds, lakes, and reservoirs. Desert kings can be abundant in the vicinity of cattle tanks and seem to be increasing steadily in numbers in irrigated agricultural areas.

Range: This kingsnake ranges westward from central Texas through New Mexico to southeastern Arizona into northern Mexico. It intergrades with the California kingsnakes and Mexican black kingsnakes in Arizona and extreme northern Mexico and with the speckled kingsnake in Texas, Oklahoma, and Kansas.

The Mexicana Complex Kingsnakes

The Gray-Banded, Variable, and Ruthven's Kingsnakes

The taxonomy and exact relationships of these three kingsnakes remains somewhat muddled. Although once considered a subspecies of the

This gray mole kingsnake was found in a north Florida garden.

variable kingsnake, *L. mexicana*, the gray-banded kingsnake is now afforded its own full-species status. Likewise, Ruthven's kingsnake has been elevated to a full species from *L. triangulum*. However, there now seems little question that all are in the *L. mexicana* complex.

Lampropeltis mexicana, once subspecifically diverse, has been purged of all races. The color forms on which the subspecies were based have been found not to be geographically oriented as was once surmised. In fact, all phases may be hatched from the same clutch of eggs. References to the races *mexicana, greeri, leonis,* and *thayeri* are therefore invalid.

These three beautiful kingsnakes are coveted by hobbyist collectors. Of the three, only the gray-banded kingsnake occurs in the United States. Both the variable and the Ruthven's kingsnakes are of Mexican distribution. Albinos of the variable and Ruthven's kingsnakes have been produced but those of the gray-banded kingsnake have not. To date, advertised albino gray-bands are actually hybrids.

Gray-Banded Kingsnake
Lampropeltis alterna
(Brown, 1901)

Range: This variable snake ranges southward from western Texas and immediately adjacent New Mexico to the Mexican states of Durango and Nuevo Leon. It is a denizen of aridlands and semiaridlands, where it seeks shelter in rock-cuts, escarpments, and canyons.

Color: There are two distinctly different color phases and many intermediates.

Blair's phase: This phase is so different in appearance from the gray-banded phase that it was once afforded its own subspecific designation. At its brightest, this is a four-color snake. The ground color is very light olive gray. It has broad, bright red saddles that are broadly edged with black, the black being narrowly edged with lighter gray or off-white. At its darkest, the ground color is a very dark storm-gray, the red saddles are reduced in breadth, the black edging is proportionately wider, and the light gray outer saddle margins are very prominent. Intermediate phases are commonly found.

Gray-banded phase: This phase seems the more stable. The gray ground color is patterned by black saddles (often bearing a little red or orange in the center) on the neck and tail. Between these are alternating complete and broken rings of black. Occasional intermediates between the two phases are found.

Although known, full striping (rather than saddles) is very rare, but partial anterior striping is more common. This tendency seems more predominant on the Blair's phase examples.

Eggs: Up to 14 eggs have been reported in a single clutch.

Once immensely popular in the hobby, of late the market for gray-banded kingsnakes seems to have plateaued.

Variable Kingsnake
Lampropeltis mexicana
(Garman, 1884)

This is another of the kingsnake species where hobbyist usage of outdated subspecific names continues. Since this is a hobbyist's book, we will use these names but will place them in quotation marks.

Color: *"San Luis Potosi, 'mexicana' phase:"* This variable snake usually has large, rather squared, black-edged, red dorsal saddles. The black may be thinly bordered on its outside edge with white. The red may vary from dull to bright and in superficial appearance the snakes at one end of the spectrum may look rather like our eastern milksnake, while those at the opposite extreme appear rather similar to the gray-banded kingsnake. The bands are gray, the nose is gray, and the head markings are red. The nape blotch is in the form of a Y with the forks directed anteriorly. The belly is blotched with black.

Range: The primary range of this phase are the mountainous areas surrounding the Chihuahua Desert as well as restricted mountainous regions in the Mexican states of Tamaulipas, San Luis Potosi, Coahuila, Nuevo Leon, Guanajuato, Zacatecas, and Durango.

Color: *"Durango Mountain, 'greeri' phase:"* The white-bordered, black "saddles" are quite restricted, often in the form of diamonds, and may lack red centers. The background coloration is usually lighter than that of the previous phase, being light gray to buff. The nose is gray; black markings occur on the head. The nape blotch is lengthened but is not usually in the form of a Y, having instead a convex anterior margin. Some of the dark belly blotches may be divided by an "indistinct light stripe."

Range: This phase occurs in mountains of the Mexican state of Durango.

Color: *"Variable, 'thayeri' phase:"* In color, this phase may be like either of the phases of this species mentioned above, may near the colors and pattern of either the gray-banded or the Ruthven's kingsnakes, or may display many other combinations. Among the additional combinations are dorsal markings reduced to short crossbars and ground colors that vary between pearl gray, warm buff, or pale cream. Albinos, melanistics, and every other imaginable color variation have been seen. The head may be mostly gray or buff, or prominently marked with red, black, or both.

Range: This phase occurs only on the eastern slope of the Mexican Plateau in the Maquihauna area of Tamaulipas.

Color: *"Nuevo Leon or 'leonis' phase":* This is a color phase of the variable kingsnake. Hobbyist usage restricts the colors of this phase to an orange to cream ground color that is marked dorsally with very narrow, white-bordered, black-edged bands of warm orange. In all phases, the large eye has a yellowish brown iris.

Eggs: Up to a dozen eggs may be produced in a single clutch. Healthy females may double clutch.

Size: Although usually smaller, variable kingsnakes may slightly exceed, a 3 foot (91 cm) total length.

Queretaro (Ruthven's) Kingsnake

Lampropeltis ruthveni
(Blanchard, 1920)

Range: This is a snake of the Central Mexican Plateau. It occurs in the states of Jalisco, Queretaro, and Michoacan, inhabiting rocky, wooded uplands.

Color: The Queretaro kingsnake is quite like a "typical" milksnake in pattern and color. At first glance, *L. ruthveni* would appear to be a red, black, and white-banded snake. However, unlike *triangulum* complex milksnakes, all bands are separated by a barely discernable outline of lime green. Both the red and white bands tend to be tan on the belly. The broad, distinct head of *L. ruthveni* is black with some red or tan areas present. Albino specimens of the Queretaro kingsnake are now readily available.

Eggs: Up to a dozen eggs may be produced by a healthy female.

Size: Although some specimens have attained 36 inches (91 cm) in overall length, most adults are about 6 inches (15 cm) shorter.

Sonoran Mountain Kingsnakes

Lampropeltis pyromelana
(Cope, 1886)

Range: These snakes occur in pine, fir, and oak forests at elevations between 3,000 and 9,000 feet (914–2,743 m). An herbaceous undercover may be sparse or thick. It has been found that many of the characteristics used to identify subspecies overlap, rendering race differentiations difficult to impossible to ascertain.

Hobbyists continue to recognize four races, of which one, *L. p. knoblochi*, is a Mexican endemic.

Red phase mole kings do not occur as commonly as the gray phase.

Care: The care for all is identical. To cycle these snakes for breeding, a period of brumation (hibernation) is necessary.

Size: All attain lengths of 36 to 44 inches (91–112 cm).

Eggs: Clutches contain from four to nine eggs. These are easily kept snakes that are quite popular with hobbyists. The greatest demand would seem to be for the small, very supple, and brightly colored Chihuahua race, *L. p. knoblochi.* Albinos and aberrant patterns have now been developed.

Arizona Mountain Kingsnake

Lampropeltis pyromelana pyromelana
(Cope, 1886)

This beautiful and slender snake is the most widely distributed of the four subspecies of *L. pyromelana.*

Color: It has 10 infralabial scales on each side of its lower jaw. This subspecies is somewhat variable in color but can be darker than the other races. The light rings usually number 43 or more on the body (and about a dozen more on the tail); they can vary from white to buff in color. The red rings can be narrow or wide and may be either entire or broken dorsally by black pigment. The red markings are usually of a triangular shape with the apex directed dorsally. Old specimens may develop a suffusion of dark pigment middorsally. The snout of this race is often darker than those of the other races, being either white or buff but containing at least some darker pigment.

Range: This subspecies is found in northern Chihuahua and Sonora, Mexico, then northward in suitable habitat through much of eastern and central Arizona.

Huachuca Mountain Kingsnake

Lampropeltis pyromelana woodini
(Tanner, 1953)

Color: There are usually 10 infralabials scales. White body rings number from 37 to 42, the snout bears less dark pigment, and the red rings may be a bit brighter and wider than those of the closely allied *L. p. pyromelana* when compared.

Range: The range of this subspecies is restricted to the Huachuca Mountains of southern Arizona and adjacent Mexico.

Utah Mountain Kingsnake

Lampropeltis pyromelana infralabialis
(Tanner, 1953)

Color: The central portion of the head is black. A white ring is present on the posterior third of the head. This is broader at its base than middorsally. This race has only nine infralabials scales.

Florida kingsnakes are dark as babies and may have red on their flanks.

The white ring count on the body varies from 42 to 57 with an additional 9 to 12 white rings on the tail.

Range: This snake is rarely found at elevations lower than 5,500 feet (1,676 m). Habitats near permanent streams are preferred. This, the most northerly race of the Sonoran mountain kingsnake occurs in at least four disjunct ranges in northern Arizona, eastern Nevada and western Utah. This race is not common in collections and continues to command high prices when it is offered for sale.

Chihuahua Mountain Kingsnake

Lampropeltis pyromelana knoblochi
(Taylor, 1940)

This rather small subspecies of the Sonoran mountain kingsnake is considered the prettiest by many hobbyists. Unlike the other three races of *pyromelana*, all of which are active by day in suitable weather, the Chihuahua mountain kingsnake is said to be more crepuscular and nocturnal.

Color: The head of this race bears more white than the heads of the other forms do. The white temporal band often connects with the white of the snout beneath the eyes. The red markings may be broken dorsally by black pigment and also be separated from the red of the belly plates by a black ventrolateral stripe. There are about 44 white rings on the body and an additional dozen or so on the tail.

Size: The record size, for a specimen that has survived more than 17 years as a captive (and is still breeding!) is 42 inches (102 cm).

Because of collecting restrictions currently in place in Mexico, there are comparatively few breeding specimens of *L. p. knoblochi* in American collections. The demand for babies of this race, therefore, continues to outpace the number available. Because of this, the prices of those that do become available are usually quite high.

Range: This coveted serpent is restricted in distribution to the Mojarachic region of Chihuahua, Mexico.

Milksnakes

Lampropeltis triangulum
(Lacepede, 1788)

Of the several groups of kingsnakes, the milksnakes are by far the most diverse. Colors, sizes, morphologies, patterns, and habitat preferences all vary tremendously. Milksnakes have the largest range of any American snake. They are found in one or the other of their 24 races from southeastern Canada to Ecuador. The most frequently seen combination of colors joins black, white, or yellow, and red or orange in precisely arranged rings, bands, or saddles. Some of the subspecies are confusingly similar and will be difficult to identify if geographic origin is not known.

Most milksnakes are hardy, easily cared for, and beautifully colored. Except for the continual array of newly developed patterns and colors, most milksnakes are now bred in great numbers and are very affordable.

Among these snakes, as much because of the genetic plasticity as for any other reason, the Mexican milk, the Pueblan milk, and the Honduran milksnakes are the hands-down hobbyist favorites. One-time favorites such as the "Coastal Plains" milk, the scarlet kingsnake, and the Sinaloan milksnake now trail far behind.

Color: Albino specimens of eastern milksnakes, Nelson's milksnakes, Honduran milksnakes, and scarlet kingsnakes have been found. Pastel phases of the Louisiana milksnake and the scarlet kingsnake are known. Apricot Pueblan milksnakes and a neon-purple Louisiana milksnake are also known. Bispecific and trispecific and even more convoluted genetic anomalies are now commonplace. Depending on the race, hatchlings may be less, equally, or more colorful than the adults.

Many of these secretive snakes retain an aversion to being handled. If restrained or surprised, many whip enthusiastically from side to side and will empty cloacal contents while doing so. This can be disconcerting for a squeamish handler.

Milksnakes of the United States

Eastern Milksnake

Lampropeltis triangulum triangulum
(Lacepede, 1788)

This is the only milksnake to occur in Canada. Because it is also one of the least colorful, it is not in great hobbyist demand.

Color: This snake has a Y or a V rather than a ring as the first marking posterior to the head. The pattern consists of 26 to 54 dorsal blotches or saddles and alternating lateral spots. In color these vary from reddish brown to gray and have black borders. This is a snake of prairies, open woodlands, bogs, fields, lakes, rural farmlands, and even littoral locations. It particularly favors stream edges, rocky forested hillsides, and barn areas where amphibians and rodents abound.

Size: Adult eastern milksnakes may near 5 feet (152 cm) in length but are usually considerably smaller.

Range: This race ranges from extreme southeastern Canada, southward to Alabama,

Tennessee, Georgia, North Carolina, Illinois, and Kentucky.

Louisiana Milksnake

Lampropeltis triangulum amaura
(Cope, 1861)

Despite its beauty, this tricolor is not in great hobbyist demand.

Color: The bands may or may not cross the belly. If broken ventrally, the wide red bands are often completely encircled with black. The white bands may appear slightly grayed dorsally. The snout is light and may be grayish white to red, or, rarely, entirely black.

Size: This is a smaller subspecies of the milksnake that rarely exceeds 26 inches (80 cm) in total length. Hatchlings are only about 5 inches (13 cm) long.

Range: Besides the entire state of Louisiana (with the exception of the bayou country in the extreme south), this snake occurs in southern Arkansas, southeastern Oklahoma, and eastern Texas.

Mexican Milksnake

Lampropeltis triangulum annulata
(Kennicott, 1861)

Color: This pretty milksnake is popular with hobbyists. The venter is predominantly black. White mottling may be visible on the internasals and anterior supralabials. Black tipping does not occur on the yellow or red scales. Red markings, which are in the form of extensive saddles (they are interrupted midventrally by black) rather than rings, number between 14 and 20. Old specimens tend to be a shade or two darker than young ones.

Range: Found predominantly in Tamaulipas, central Nuevo Leon, and southern and eastern Coahuila, Mexico, this milksnake is also fairly common in southern Texas. Because of the excessive daytime heat in their preferred semi-arid habitats, it is primarily nocturnal during the summer months. Mexican milksnakes occur at altitudes between sea level and 4,000 feet (1,200 m).

Size: They attain a length of 24 to 30 inches (61–76 cm).

Hatchlings: The hatchlings are about 8 inches (20 cm) in length and are robust enough to accept newly born pinky mice for their first meal. This milksnake is commonly bred in captivity and many pattern aberrancies have been established.

New Mexico Milksnake

Lampropeltis triangulum celaenops
(Stejneger, 1903)

Color: Colloquially referred to as the "Big Bend milksnake," this race has a white-flecked black nose. Its head is also black as far back as the posterior one-third of the parietal scales. The first white band is wide and prominent. The 17 to 25 pale red bands are the widest. The areas of black are narrower than the white. There is no black tipping on the red or white scales.

Size: This snake attains a length of 24 inches (61 cm). It inhabits juniper woodlands, oak forests, and gamma grass areas at elevations of up to 6,900 feet (2,090 m).

Diet: The primary diet of wild specimens consists of lizards (Sceloporus). Some captive specimens are reluctant to accept mice and, at 6 inches (15 cm) in length, the hatchlings may be too small to do so. You may have to resort to some of the "tricks of the trade" to work this form over to an easily procured diet.

Eastern black kingsnakes are the darkest of the eastern subspecies.

Range: This milksnake is well known from Texas' Big Bend region westward to eastern Arizona.

Scarlet Kingsnake

Lampropeltis triangulum elapsoides
(Holbrook, 1838)

This 24-inch-long (60-cm) lampropeltine of the southeastern United States is, perhaps, the most divergent of the milksnakes. It is a slender, narrow-headed burrower that ascends into positions behind the loosened bark in dead but still standing trees during the spring when ground water levels are high.

Color: This is a brilliantly colored snake that is precisely and immaculately ringed in red, black, and yellow (the yellow is white on hatchlings and juveniles).

Diet: The small size and narrowness of the head prevents this snake from eating all but small lizards (they prefer ground skinks and the smallest nestling mice). Although it is occasionally captive bred, most pet trade examples are wild-collected.

Range: It may be found in mixed woodlands but can be abundant in pine woods.

Central Plains Milksnake

Lampropeltis triangulum gentilis
(Baird and Girard, 1853)

Color: This common milksnake is patterned with an average of 30 black-edged red to orange saddles. The ground color is light gray to off white. The snout is light with dark mottling. The black crown extends rearward nearly to the posterior edge of the parietal scales. The base of the white temporal band may extend forward to a point beneath the eye. This is a snake of rocky prairies, savannas, canyons, and rock-strewn slopes. It can be very common where conditions are ideal.

Size: The 18 to 24 inch (46–61 cm) adults are hardy and easily cared for, readily accepting fuzzy mice. The 5.5 to 6 inch (14–15 cm) hatchlings can be a challenge to feed.

Range: This snake ranges eastward from eastern Colorado and the Texas Panhandle to south-central Nebraska and central and western Kansas.

Pale Milksnake

Lampropeltis triangulum multistriata
(Kennicott, 1861)

Color: This aptly named milksnake has 22 to 32 black-edged orange (rather than red) saddles. The snout is light (often a very pale orange) and is flecked with dark pigment. The dark markings are often the most prevalent at the edges of the prefrontals, the internasals, and the rostral. Both the belly and the light banding is pale gray to off white.

Size: The adult size is about 30 inches (76 cm) in length. Hatchlings measure only about 6 inches (15 cm) in length.

Range: This is a secretive snake of the dunes and prairies of Nebraska, southwestern South Dakota, Wyoming, and Montana. It is occasionally captive bred, but has not become truly popular.

Red Milksnake

Lampropeltis triangulum syspila
(Cope, 1888)

This is a pretty, hardy, and common milksnake.

Color: The 16 to 31 red saddles are bordered with black. Some lateral spotting is generally present. The snout and anterior portion of the head is white; the top of the head is red. The white temporal band is rather narrow and the base is expanded both anteriorly and posteriorly. The venter is white with scattered, but prominent, black spotting.

Range: This milksnake inhabits open woodlands, rocky, grass-covered hillsides, the environs of streams and other watercourses, and irrigated agricultural areas over a vast region from southern Indiana and western Kentucky westward to eastern Oklahoma and extreme southeastern South Dakota.

A narrow white chain pattern is typical of most eastern kingsnakes.

Size: At 30 to 42 inches (75-107 cm) adults are sufficiently large to overpower and eat small adult mice. Both adults and hatchlings are easily kept and usually eat readily.

Utah Milksnake

Lampropeltis triangulum taylori
(Tanner and Loomis, 1957)

This 30-inch-long (76-cm) subspecies ranges further west than any other U.S. milksnake. It is poorly represented in captive collections.

Color: Although the nose of some specimens may be entirely black, that of others is extensively patterned with light pigment. In general appearance, this race looks much like a busily patterned New Mexico milksnake with 23 to 34 black-edged red saddles, and often, greater amounts of white. Some of the red saddles may be interrupted by black pigment vertebrally. The venter is pale gray.

Range: This milksnake is found in northeastern or central Utah and western Colorado. Small, disjunct populations of what might be this race occur in northcentral and northeastern Arizona.

"Coastal Plains Intergrade" Milksnake

Lampropeltis t. triangulum x *L. t. elapsoides*

This is beautiful snake with a problematic lineage. The parental forms are thought to be the eastern milksnake and the scarlet kingsnake. Hobbyist breeders continue to refer to the snake as *L. t. temporalis*. This snake is popular with hobbyists and striped patterns have been developed.

Size: This milksnake averages 21 to 35 inches (53–89 cm) in length but occasionally nears 40 inches (102 cm).

Color: It has a well-defined light collar and a dorsal pattern of 24 to 31 black-edged red saddles. The anterior saddles reach the ventral scales. Prominent lateral blotches are lacking. The ground color is whitish or white with the vaguest of yellow tinges. The top of the head is red. The venter is off white with black blotches.

Range: This beautiful snake inhabits bogs, fields, and open woodlands from central New Jersey to southeastern Pennsylvania, Delaware, Maryland, the Shenandoah Valley of Virginia, and extreme northeastern North Carolina.

Milksnakes of Latin America

Guatemala Milksnake

Lampropeltis triangulum abnorma
(Bocourt, 1866)

Size: This is a 5-foot-long (152-cm) milksnake of variable color and pattern.

Color: Most are typically marked with black, white, and red rings but a few may lack most or all of the white. If white is present, the rings are only two scale rows wide and the scales are heavily tipped with black. The red rings are often incomplete and broken by black pigment middorsally. This race has a black-tipped snout followed by a broad white band, which is, in turn, followed, by a broad black temporal band, then another band of black.

Range: This snake of forest and savanna habitats ranges from northeastern Chips, Mexico, to central and northwestern Guatemala and northwestern Honduras. It has not gained popularity with hobbyists.

Andean Milksnake

Lampropeltis triangulum andesiana
(Williams, 1978)

This is one of the two largest forms of milksnake. It has become regularly available in the pet trade.

Color: The red and white scales are often (but not invariably) prominently tipped with black. Adults are usually duller than the juveniles. Some adults are of almost dusky appearance. The white snout scales of this subspecies have black sutures and there is usually a considerable amount of white on the cheeks. The chin is predominantly light. The 24 to 32 red rings may be interrupted by black middorsally and may not fully cross the venter.

Like other milksnakes, *andesiana* is known to intergrade with abutting races.

Size and range: This huge milksnake (to more than 66 inches [168 cm]) occurs in the Colombian Andes where its altitudinal preferences are from 733–9,000 feet (220–2,700 m). Hatchlings measure about 9 inches (23 cm).

Jalisco Milksnake

Lampropeltis triangulum arcifera
(Werner, 1903)

Color: This milksnake has both a black snout and head. The snout may have scattered flecks of white. The anterior edge of the first white ring angles forward to touch the corner of the mouth. Neither the white nor the red scales are tipped with black. The 14 to 31 red rings may be interrupted middorsally by black scales.

Range: This is a snake of the arid tropical scrub, mesquite grasslands, and pine oak woodlands of the western Mexican plateau in the states of Morelos, Guerrero, Jalisco, Queretaro, Hidalgo, and Michoacan.

Size: Adults reach 42 inches (107 cm) in length. This milksnake has been captive bred but it is not commonly available to hobbyists.

Blanchard's (Yucatan) Milksnake

Lampropeltis triangulum blanchardi
(Stuart, 1935)

This subspecies is a rarity in captivity.

Color: The black of the nose and head projects rearward midcranially, intersecting the prominent yellow temporal band and connecting with the first black band. Both the yellow and the red scales are often tipped with black. There are 14 to 20 red rings.

Range: Mexico's Yucatan Peninsula is home to this snake. Habitats include lush deciduous forests and xeric and thorn scrub-covered savannas.

Size: Adults attain a length of 36 to 42 inches (91–107 cm).

Pueblan Milksnake

Lampropeltis triangulum campbelli
(Quinn, 1983)

The Pueblan milksnake has become one of the two most commonly seen of the Mexican subspecies.

Color: It is of variable color. Most examples have broad bands of jet black, pure white, and bright red, all of identical width. This unusual arrangement distinguishes this subspecies from all other milksnakes. The black snout bears a white U, the top directed anteriorly, on the prefrontals and frontal. There are an average of 16 red rings, 32 black rings, and 16 white body rings. The tail has 5 black and 5 white rings but lacks red. The first white ring behind the head is normally very broad and selected breeding has broadened it even more. Pueblan milks with this broadened white marking are termed "sockheads." An attractive "apricot" phase has been developed and specimens lacking all traces of red are now being bred. Prices have dropped dramatically but vary according to the color and the pattern of the snake.

Size: The Pueblan milksnake may attain a length of 3 feet (90 cm) but is usually a few inches smaller. The robust hatchlings are about 9 inches (23 cm) and well able (and usually more than ready!) to eat pink mice for their first meal.

Range: This snake occurs in southern Puebla, eastern Morelos, and northern Oaxaca, Mexico.

Conant's Milksnake

Lampropeltis triangulum conanti
(Williams, 1978)

This subspecies remains one of the rarest milksnakes in captivity.

Color: The broad red rings number 11 to 20. The black are narrow and the yellow is very reduced and may be spots rather than rings. The red scales often have a small degree of black tipping. The nose and head are black. The black of the head may connect with the first black band. The temporal area contains large and well defined spots of yellow-ocher.

Albino Huachuca Mountain kingsnakes are well known in the hobby.

The Peninsula Florida intergrade kingsnake is abundant in the sugarcane and sod fields of the southern peninsula.

Range: This is a snake of tropical deciduous forests to rocky pine oak woodlands at elevations of 5,600 feet (1,707 m) in the Sierra Madre del Sur of Guerrero and Oaxaca Mexico.

Adults attain a length of about 46 inches (117 cm).

Dixon's Milksnake

Lampropeltis triangulum dixoni
(Quinn, 1983)

This is an infrequently seen snake.

Color: It has an average of 20 dark red rings on the body and 5 yellow bands on the tail. Although they are the widest, nearly all of the red rings are interrupted both dorsally and ventrally by extensions of the black rings. The light bands are narrow. The snout and anterior top of the head are black.

Range: Dixon's milksnake inhabits mountain passes and valleys in the Mexican state of San Luis Potosi and in the Jalapan Valley of north-eastern Queretaro.

Size: An adult length of about 42 inches (107 cm) is attained.

Black Milksnake

Lampropeltis triangulum gaigeae
(Dunn, 1937)

Color: Although typically tricolored (red, black, and yellow; an average of 20 red bands) at hatching, this high-altitude Costa Rican and Panamanian milksnake usually becomes entirely black at adulthood. The suffusion of black pigment starts as black scale. Once begun, the darkening progresses with each

Hobbyists call desert kingsnakes with elongated black head markings "sockheads."

skin shedding. It is surmised that the dark coloration aids in thermoregulation.

Range: This milksnake occurs in moist montane forest habitats at altitudes between 5,000 and 7,400 feet (1,500–2,220 m).

Size: Adults in excess of 5 feet (1.5 m) in length have been recorded.

Honduran Milksnake

Lampropeltis triangulum hondurensis
(Williams, 1978)

Color: This huge milksnake is readily available in three distinctly different natural color phases. About a dozen genetically engineered colors and patterns are also now available. The three normal morphs are the tricolored (red, black, and yellow), the bicolored (black and red) and the tangerine (fire orange and black). Genetically engineered morphs include, among others, albinos, snows, pinstriped, calicos, piebald, and anerythristic.

In appearance the tricolored morph is quite typical. There are 14 to 26 red bands. The rostral area is black but the rest of the snout is red. The dark eyeband is wide and the light temporal band expands widely at the base. If black tipping does occur on the red scales it is usually minimal. The bicolored phase has broad red rings and narrower black ones. The red scales are often tipped with black. The tangerine may be of only moderate brilliance, but some examples are spectacularly bright in color. The best among them have wide bands of intense red-orange framing narrow black bands that encompass a band of paler tangerine-orange.

Cost: While the cost of average specimens is rather low, that of the newer developed morphs can reach high into the hundreds of dollars.

Range: This snake occurs at elevations between sea level and 400 feet (120 m) in the countries of Nicaragua, the Caribbean slope of Honduras, and probably in northeastern Costa Rica.

Size: It attains an adult size of more than 5 feet (1.5 m). Hatchlings are large enough to eat pinky mice.

Ecuadorian Milksnake
Lampropeltis triangulum micropholis
(Cope, 1861)

Size: At an adult length of slightly more than 6 feet (183 cm), this is one of the two largest milksnakes.

Range: This snake occurs at lower elevations southward from the Canal Zone and eastern Panama to southcentral Ecuador, then eastward to the Rio Magdalena Valley of Colombia and the Cordillera de la Costa of Venezuela.

Color: The tip of the snout is dark. A white band is present anterior to the eyes. The black eyeband is wide. The temporal band is narrow and widens noticeably at its base. The red bands are about the same width as the triads that contain the yellow or white. There is often a minimal amount of black tipping on the red dorsal scales, but the tipping may become more prominent laterally. The red body rings number between 10 and 18. This is not yet a commonly seen milksnake.

Nelson's Milksnake
Lampropeltis triangulum nelsoni
(Blanchard, 1920)

Color: This milksnake has 13 to 18 red rings and usually a dark-flecked light snout (but rarely the snout may be predominantly black). The red bands are very wide, the black dramatically less so, and the white is very narrow. There is virtually no black tipping on either the red or the white scales. Albinism and pattern aberrancies are now established.

Range: This is a milksnake of semiarid coastal thorn scrub and interior tropical deciduous forests of southern Guanajuato and central Jalisco to the Pacific Coast. It may be found on the narrow plains of northwestern Michoacan and also on the Tres Marias Islands. The distribution of Nelson's milksnake seems tied to the presence of water courses, including those affiliated with irrigation and agricultural projects.

Size: The average adult length is 42 inches (107 cm).

Pacific American Milksnake
Lampropeltis triangulum oligozona
(Bocourt, 1886)

Size and range: This milksnake of Oaxaca's Pacific slope, adjacent Chiapas, and Guatemala can reach 42 inches (107 cm) in total length.

Color: It has a black head and snout. A distinct white or yellow wedge, apex directed rearward, appears on the internasals and prefrontals. Both the red and white scales are distinctly tipped with black. The red rings number between 10 and 16. It is uncommon in the pet trade.

Atlantic Central American Milksnake
Lampropeltis triangulum polyzona
(Cope, 1861)

This is another of the several Mexican milksnakes that would be virtually impossible to identify without field data.

Color: The head and snout (except for the nasals and anterior supralabials, which are white), is black. The white temporal band involves the very posterior section of the parietals, extends down the sides of the head, and expands far forward at its base. The red body rings number from 16 to 22.

Range: This is an uncommon species of low-land tropical rain forest habitats in the Mexican states of Veracruz, San Luis Potosi, and Tabasco. It has been recorded at elevations of up to 6,000 feet (1,828 m). It is not common in the pet trade.

Size: Adults are from 42 to 60 inches (109–152 cm) long.

Sinaloan Milksnake

Lampropeltis triangulum sinaloae
(Williams, 1978)

This is one of the most beautiful of all milk-snakes.

Color: All (10 to 16) of the very wide red rings completely encircle the body. Neither the red nor the white scales bear black tipping. Both the black and the white rings are proportionately narrow. Except for the white nasals, the nose and head are mostly black. The temporal band is prominent and complete. This is one of the most commonly bred of the tricolors and many aberrant colors (including albinos) and patterns are now available.

Size: Adults attain a length of 4 feet (122 cm).

Diet: Adults usually feed voraciously and the 10-inch (26-cm) hatchlings are able to easily consume newly born mice.

Range: This milksnake is common in the low-lands of Sinaloa as well as being present in southwestern Sonora and eastward up the valley of the Rio Fuerte into southwestern Chihuahua.

Smith's Milksnake

Lampropeltis triangulum smithi
(Williams, 1978)

The identification of this milksnake must be based primarily on geographic origin.

Color: The red body rings number between 19 and 30 and the red scales may or may not have black tipping. The white scales tend to have a moderate amount of black tipping. The head is black with a large white or mottled black on white snout area. The venter has extensive black pigment.

Habitat: Habitats include tropical forests, valleys, passes, and plains in the Sierra Madre Oriental from southeastern San Luis Potosi, south through Queretaro, Hidalgo, Puebla, and into the Jalapa area of Veracruz, Mexico.

Size: Adult size is 3.5 feet (107 cm).

Stuart's Milksnake

Lampropeltis triangulum stuarti
(Williams, 1978)

Range: The diagnostic V (apex rearward) on the snout is an excellent fieldmark for this Pacific slope, dry forest and coastal plain resident of El Salvador, Honduras, Nicaragua, and northwestern Costa Rica.

Size: Adults of this race can exceed 46 inches (117 cm) in length.

Color: The scales in the 19 to 28 red body rings (as well as the white scales) may or may not be moderately tipped with black.

Imported specimens are occasionally available in the American pet market but this has not become a popular milksnake.

California Mountain Kingsnakes

Lampropeltis zonata
(Lockington, 1876)

Range: Of the seven subspecies of the California mountain kingsnake, five occur in our three Pacific Coast states and two are restricted in distribution to Mexico's Baja peninsula area. All occur in disjunct populations. Specimens have been found at elevations of nearly 9,000 feet

This is a pretty Florida kingsnake from Dade County, Florida.

(2,750 m) but some also occur at sea level. Captive specimens from higher elevations generally do better in cooler climates and environments.

Size: Although some may occasionally attain a length of 4 feet (122 cm), most are adult at 24 to 30 inches (61–76 cm).

Albinos of Queretaro kingsnakes are well established in herpetoculture.

Diet: The small size of many California mountain kingsnakes restricts their diet to small lizards and nestling rodents. Large specimens are perfectly capable—and more than willing—of overpowering and consuming fully grown mice. In the wild, salamanders, tiny anurans, smaller snakes, and an occasional nestling of a ground-nesting bird species will round out the diet.

Color: Despite being a "tricolored" species, with advancing age many specimens show an increase in black pigment and a corresponding decrease in red. Colors and patterns vary even within populations. On some the white may be gray and the red may be orange. The Todos Santos Island kingsnake is the most extreme in color differences with the red lacking entirely or being reduced to only a few scales on the lower sides.

Traditionally the number of "triads" that contain red has been important in differentiating subspecies. (A "triad" is a set of black rings between which a red and/or scales are usually present.) However, it has been found that many of the supposed differences actually overlap, and geographic location may be the most important identifying feature. Where abutting ranges allow two races to intergrade and produce a melding of characteristics even geography may not help.

Eggs: Many of the races have been bred in captivity but few aberrancies have been reported. A clutch usually contains 8 or fewer eggs.

Saint Helena Mountain Kingsnake

Lampropeltis zonata zonata
(Lockington, 1876)

This, the nominate form, is poorly known. This race is known to be secretive and thought to be rare.

The white bands of the Mexican milksnake yellow with age.

Color: It has from 24 to 30 body triads and more than 50 percent of the red bands are complete. Both the white and the black bands are wide, hence the red bands are correspondingly narrow.

Range: In its purest form, the Saint Helena mountain kingsnake occurs in Mendocino, Napa, and Sonoma counties, California. Intergrades occur as far north as southcentral Washington and adjacent Oregon and near White Salmon, Washington.

Sierra Mountain Kingsnake
Lampropeltis zonata multicincta
(Yarrow, 1882)

This is actually one of the larger and (usually) more brightly colored races of the California mountain kingsnake. It is unquestionably a hobbyist favorite.

Color: A black-nosed variety, the posterior edge of the first white band is located behind the corner of the mouth. Specimens in some populations may lack all traces of red, instead being only black and white. There are 23 to 48 body triads present.

Size: At 47⅜ inches (119 cm), the largest of the specimens maintained at the Chaffee Zoo in Fresno, California, reminded me of a very, very hefty, broom handle-sized candy cane.

Range: The range of the Sierra mountain kingsnake includes the Sierra Nevada Mountains from Kern and Tulare Counties, north to Shasta County, California. It also occurs in southwestern Oregon where it intergrades with the Saint Helena mountain kingsnake.

Coastal Mountain Kingsnake
Lampropeltis zonata multifasciata
(Bocourt, 1886)

Color: Many examples of this brightly colored subspecies have considerable red coloration on the snout and most have fewer than 41 body triads. The black bands are usually narrow, the red bands are broad. The rear edge of the first white band may be either behind or anterior to the corner of the mouth.

Range: This subspecies occurs both at sea level and in montane habitats from south of San Francisco, south to the Santa Clara River in Ventura County, California.

San Bernardino Mountain Kingsnake

Lampropeltis zonata parvirubra
(Zweifel, 1952)

Color: This subspecies has a black snout and (except for the temporal area) head. It has between 35 and 48 (average 41) body triads. The black areas predominate. More than half of the red bands completely cross the dorsum. The posterior margin of the first white band is located on or just anterior to the last upper labial.

Range: Look for this subspecies in the foothills and canyons of southern California's Los Angeles, San Bernardino, and central Riverside counties.

San Diego Mountain Kingsnake

Lampropeltis zonata pulchra
(Zweifel, 1952)

Color: This subspecies differs from the San Bernardino mountain kingsnake primarily in that it has fewer than 38 triads on its body. The posterior edge of the first white band is located either on or just anterior to the last upper labial scale. Well over half of the red bands completely cross the dorsum. This is a very colorful race that is much desired by the collectors of tricolors. It is now being captive bred in some numbers and is considered one of the easier subspecies to maintain and breed in captivity.

Range: This snake occurs in Los Angeles, Orange, Riverside, and San Diego counties in southern California.

San Pedro Mountain Kingsnake

Lampropeltis zonata agalma
(Van Denburgh and Slevin, 1923)

Size: This small subspecies seldom attains a length of more than 30 inches (76 cm). Hatchlings are about 7 inches (18 cm) in length.

Color: This is one of the more brightly colored forms, with red present in at least half of the more than 40 triads. The black nose of this pretty snake has a rather distinctive pattern of red. The red may be especially prominent at the edges of the prefrontal, frontal, and supraocular scales. The posterior edge of the first white ring is anterior to the posterior edge of the last upper labial scale.

Range: This subspecies is restricted to northern Baja California where it occurs in the Sierra Juarez and the Sierra San Pedro Martir mountains.

Hobbyists have now begun breeding this coveted subspecies in substantial numbers. An expensive and difficult to acquire race only a few years ago, *agalma* is now readily available at affordable prices.

Todos Santos Island Kingsnake

Lampropeltis zonata herrerae
(Van Denburgh and Slevin, 1923)

This is *the* black and white mountain kingsnake.

Range: It occurs only on South Todos Santos Island, off the Pacific coast of northern Baja California Norte. Few, if any, specimens are available in the pet trade.

Color: The posterior edge of the first white ring is anterior to the corner of the mouth. Because of the lack of red, this form superficially appears more like a diminutive California kingsnake than one of the California mountain kingsnakes.

Size: The average length of an adult is 24 to 30 inches (61 to 76 cm). Hatchlings measure less than 8 inches (20 cm) in total length. The natural history of this restricted form is largely unknown.

G L O S S A R Y

abdomen: lower surface of the body between the neck and the cloaca.

anal plate: scale in front of the cloaca, single or divided.

apical pit(s): sensory pits contained in the dorsal and lateral scales of some snakes.

bilobed: having two lobes.

body: the section from nape to cloaca.

cloaca: the common chamber into which the reproductive, excretory, and urinary canals deposit their contents. The cloaca opens to the outside through the vent.

Colubrid: snakes belonging to the family *Colubridae.*

dermal: relating to the skin.

dorsal: relating to the back or top side.

dorsal scales: scales on the back or top side that can be counted in a sequence to determine a subspecies or separate subspecies.

ecdysis: molting or shedding of the outside skin.

ectothermic: cold-blooded

endothermic: warm-blooded

hemipenes: paired invertible sex organs of the male.

internasals: enlarged scales or plates on the dorsal surface of the snout, posterior to the rostral and between the nasals.

lateral: referring to the sides.

middorsal: located on the medium of the center of the top of the back.

morph: a form or phase different from the normal.

nasal: the scale containing or between which the nostril opens.

neotropical: pertaining to the new world tropics.

oviparous: egg laying.

parietals: the pair of large scales on the rear of the dorsal surface of the head, posterior to the frontal scale and anterior to the small scales of the nape.

phase: a specific color or pattern different from the norm.

prenasal: the scale anterior to that which contains the nostril.

rostral: the enlarged scale on the tip of the snout.

scale rows: number of scale rows on the top or dorsal side, usually at mid-body.

sex (gender): externally determined by the shape and length of tail past the vent. Long and wide in males; short and tapered in females.

shed: synonym for ecdysis.

tail: the last part of the snake past the vent.

tricolor: the colloquial name used by hobbyists to refer to milksnakes.

vent: the external opening of the cloacal chamber.

ventral: referring to the belly.

Organizations

American Society of Ichthyologists
and Herpetologists
United States National Museum
Washington, DC 20560

Herpetologists' League, Inc.
University of Oklahoma
Box 478
Oklahoma City, OK 73111

Society for the Study of Amphibians
and Reptiles
Zoology Department
Ohio University
Athens, OH 45701

American Federation of Herpetoculturists
P.O. Box 300067
Escondido, CA 92030-0067

Chicago Herpetological Society
2001 North Clark Street
Chicago, IL 60614

Publications and Magazines

Captive Breeding
P.O. Box 87100
Canton, MI 48187

Reptile and Amphibian Magazine
RD 3, Box 3709-A
Pottsville, PA 17901

Reptiles
P.O. Box 6050
Mission Viejo, CA 92690

Reptilian Magazine
Mantella Publishing
22 Firs Close
Hazlemere
High Wycombe
Bucks HP15 7TF England

Vivarium
P.O. Box 300067
Escondido, CA 92030-0067

Herpetology clubs exist in many larger cities. Many of these local and national associations publish newsletters or journals of variable

The San Pedro mountain kingsnake is now often seen in the hobby.

The Utah milksnake remains uncommon in the hobby.

sophistication. Check the ads in reptile magazines or with a nearby university or science/natural history museum to learn of the club nearest you.

Books

Bartlett, Richard D. *In Search of Reptiles and Amphibians.* New York: E.J. Brill, 1988.

Blanchard, F. N. *A Revision of the King Snake Genus* Lampropeltis. Bulletin of the U.S. National Museum, 1921.

Conant, Roger. *A Field Guide to Reptiles and Amphibians of Eastern North America.* Cambridge: Houghton Mifflin, 1958.

Conant, Roger and Joseph T. Collins. *Reptiles and Amphibians of Eastern/Central North America.* Boston: Houghton Mifflin, 1991.

Ernst, Carl H. and Roger W. Barbour. *Snakes of Eastern North America.* Fairfax, VA: George Mason University Press, 1989.

Kauffeld, Carl F. *Snake and Snake Hunting.* Garden City, NY: Hanover House, 1957.

Markel, Ronald G. *Kingsnakes and Milksnakes,* Neptune City, NJ: T.F.H., 1990.

McCarthy, Colin. *Reptile* (Eyewitness Books) New York: Alfred A. Knopf, 1991.

Williams, Kenneth L. *Systematics and Natural History of the American Milksnake,* Second Edition. Milwaukee Public Museum Publication, 1988.

Wright, Albert Hazen and Anna Allen Wright. *Handbook of Snakes.* Three vols. (incl. bibliog.). Ithaca, NY: Comstock, 1949.

Pages numbers set in boldface type indicate photographs.

Acknowledgments

Special thanks go to Bill Love, Rob MacInnes, and Chris McQuade for allowing us photographic opportunities and sharing with us their expertise in milksnakes and kingsnake breeding, and to Sean McKeown for sharing his thoughts and knowledge of the California Mountain kingsnake group. We owe debts of gratitude to Dennie Miller, Carl May, Dennis Cathcart, Mike Souza, Tom Tyning, to the late Gordy Johnston for companionship on field trips, and to the herpetoculturists whose dedication to their pursuit continues to lessen the impact on the wild populations of milksnakes and kingsnakes that we so love to see in the field.

These acknowledgments would be incomplete without a word of thanks to our editor, Pat Hunter, for her care, concern, and help.

Important Note

The subject of this book is the keeping and care of nonpoisonous snakes. Snake keepers should realize, however, that even the bite of a snake regarded as nonpoisonous can have harmful consequences. So see a doctor immediately after any snake bite.

Electrical appliances used in the care of snakes must carry a valid "UL approved" marking. Everyone using such equipment should be aware of the dangers involved with it. It is strongly recommended that you purchase a device that will instantly shut off the electrical current in the event of failure in the appliances or wiring.

A circuit-protection device with a similar function has to be installed by a licensed electrician.

Photo Credits

All photos © R. D. Bartlett

All inquiries should be addressed to:
Barron's Educational Series, Inc.
250 Wireless Boulevard
Hauppauge, NY 11788
www.barronseduc.com

ISBN-13: 978-0-7641-2853-0
ISBN-10: 0-7641-2853-1

Library of Congress Catalog Card No. 2005040958

Library of Congress Cataloging-in-Publication Data
Bartlett, Richard D., 1938–
    Kingsnakes and milksnakes / R. D. Bartlett & Ronald G. Markel.—[2nd ed.]
        p. cm. — (A complete pet owner's manual)
    Markel's name appears first on the earlier edition.
    Includes bibliographical references and index.
    ISBN 0-7641-2853-1
        1. Lampropeltis as pets. I. Markel, Ronald G.
    II. Title. III. Series.

SF459.S5B3725   2005
639.3'962—dc22   2005040958

Printed in China
9 8 7 6 5 4 3 2 1